*To John
enjoy
Jack 12/17*

MOSTLY ONE LINERS CAUSE I CAN'T REMEMBER TWO

MOSTLY ONE LINERS CAUSE I CAN'T REMEMBER TWO

BOOK OF SHORT, FUNNY QUIPS

BY JACK SPRING MD

Mostly One Liners Cause I Can't Remember Two...
Copyright © 2017 by Jack Spring MD

All rights reserved. No part of this book may be used or reproduced in any form, electronic or mechanical, including photocopying, recording, or scanning into any information storage and retrieval system, without written permission from the author except in the case of brief quotation embodied in critical articles and reviews.

Cover design by Taegan M. Grice
Book design by The Troy Book Makers

Printed in the United States of America

The Troy Book Makers • Troy, New York • thetroybookmakers.com

To order additional copies of this title, contact your favorite local bookstore or visit www.shoptbmbooks.com

ISBN: 978-1-61468-405-3

This book dedicated to his family that have listened patiently to these jokes many times. It is a compilation of original humor Jack has witnessed in his life as a doctor and as a member of the race. It also is peppered with classic humor of some of the America's greatest comics such as Don Rickles, Rodney Dangerfield, Red Buttons, Red Skelton, Henny Youngman, Joan Rivers, Milton Berle, Rita Rudner, Steven Wright, and Groucho Marx, just to mention a few.

He hopes you enjoy it and have as much fun reading it as he did writing it.

Milton Berle about Henny Youngman.

"The Copper Age, Bronze Age and Iron Age are a long time ago. Doc has now entered the Metal Age: Silver in his hair, Gold in his teeth and Lead in his butt. Not a winner of the Nobel Prize for literature, but a fun read."

BORIS PANTSZAROFF PHD, CHAIRMAN
Department of Metallurgy, Union College.

ACKNOWLEDGEMENTS

I would like to thank Dr Martin Strosberg, professor at Clarkson University and Union College, for graciously acting as the editor, Taegan Grice a talented graphic artist for her wondeful work and Meradith Kill at The Troy Book Makers for her help in creating this "Literary Litany of Laughter."

ONOMASTICS: Study of proper names.

APTONYMS: Funny Names that are associated with occupations. These are actual names culled from newspapers over the past 25 years.

Doctor Zoltan Ovary • *OB GYN doctor*

Doctor Dochterman • *Family Practice*

Doctor Donald Regular • *OB GYN doctor*

Doctor Brian Blades • *General Surgeon*

Doctor Clifton Brain • *Famous English neurologist*

Doctor Alden Cockburn • *Urologist*

Doctor Steve Stream • *Urologist*

Doctor Roger Organ • *Transplant Surgeon*

Doctor A.R. Colon • *Gastroenterologist*

Ronald Supena • *Attorney*

Martha Rollova • *Prostitute*

John J. Justice • *Judge*

Joy Bang • *Prostitute*

Su Yu • *Attorney*

Dora Sicko • *Nurse's aide*

Doctor B Gargle • *Dentist*

Chief William Crook • *Police Officer*

Doctor Loniden Saline • *Chemist for GE*

Constance Barker • *Dog lover*

Cardinal Sin • *Bishop in Manila*

F. J. Kidney • *Cook*

An obituary in Arizona Star newspaper reported a lady named Myrtle Cobbledick had changed her name. She had suffered with constant harassment and bullying, so she changed it to Betsy Cobbledick.

The title of this book is called *Mostly One-Liners Because Approaching My 80th Birthday, I Can't Remember Two.* Look, I would have been 81, but I was sick for year.

...

She's been depressed ever since she seeing me in 1985. (Note in my patient's medical chart)

...

Health food makes me sick.

...

Doctors are men that prescribe medicines of which they know little, to cure diseases of which they know less, for human beings of whom they know nothing. (Voltaire) Things haven't changed much.

...

When I want your opinion, I'll give it to you.

...

At age 80, I'm not worried about sex, if she dies, she dies.

...

She is so ugly she has to frisk her self at the airport.

...

He couldn't direct traffic on a one-way street.

...

It takes longer to do things when you're older. When I watch 60 Minutes, it takes me an hour and a half.

...

What do you want them to say as they are walking by your casket? I want them to say, "Look, he's moving." (Woody Allen)

...

The Chrysler Corporation named a car after my wife. It's called the Challenger.

...

When the Post Office receives a package marked fragile, it means that they throw it underhand.

...

I'll never forget the first time we met, but I'm trying. (Groucho)

...

My wife and I have spent 30 happy years together, not bad out of 50!

...

I walked into a bar one hot summer day and I said to the bartender, "I would like something tall, icy and full of gin." He yelled to the back "Hey Doris, it's for you."

...

The only reason my good buddy had children was to meet the babysitters.

...

He's a born again Christian. I think he suffered a traumatic brain injury during his rebirth.

...

My wife called 911 and the state police arrived. The officer came to the house with a German shepherd. She said to me, "That's great, they sent me a blind state trooper."

...

I met a lady friend of mine I hadn't seen a long time. She said to me, "Jack, you haven't changed at all in 20 years." "I looked this bad 20 years ago? No wonder I couldn't get a date in high school."

...

My grandson John was voted by his classmates the one most likely to return fire.

...

My old mob friend Tony has no enemies. He's killed them all.

...

Was it you or your brother that died?

...

Your socks smell so bad, they set the sprinkler system off.

...

One woman patient told me she had a hope chest. "I've seen your chest, there's no hope!" (Red Buttons)

...

If there is a mental health organization that raises money for people like you, be sure and let me know.

...

My wife has a speech impediment, once in a while she stops to breathe.

...

You say your wife can't take a joke. Jez, she took you.

...

If you're IQ slips any lower, we will have to water you twice a day.

...

Old lawyers never die they just lose their appeal.

...

You know you're old when somebody compliments you on your alligator shoes and you are barefoot.

...

TRYING TO REMOVE TOP FROM MY CHILDPROOF MEDICINE BOTTLE

My idea of happy hour is a nap on the couch from three to 4 o'clock.

. . .

I am so old, my Social Security number is three.

. . .

Old Uncle Beduch had too many drinks in the bar one night and saw this beautiful woman, went over and kissed her. She turned around slapped him and said "You insufferable drunk, horrible, ugly man." He said, "Sorry, I thought you were my wife, you certainly sound like her."

. . .

You're old when you walk downstairs and get out of breath.

...

Nowadays I look both ways before crossing a room.

...

I had a rough day, I went to button my shirt and the button fell off, I grabbed my suitcase and the handle fell off. Gosh, I am afraid to go to the bathroom. (Rodney Dangerfield)

...

When I sit in a rocking chair, I can't get it started.

...

My knees buckle and my belt won't.

...

I watch old movies saying he's dead, she's dead and so on down the list of credits. How 'bout you?

...

Everybody offers me a ride. I guess they don't want me driving.

...

They found a mummy 3000 years old. They figured he died from a heart attack because they found a note in his hand saying bet 5000 dinars on Goliath.

...

Beduch married Mrs. Wright, but he didn't realize her first name was Always.

...

At my age, I'm a sex symbol for women that don't care anymore.

...

This service in the restaurant was so slow, I came to cut down on my drinking.

...

The Ellis Hospital wanted me to donate more money to the building fund. "Look, my mother needs 24 hour care, my brother is on welfare and my daughter is being evicted from her apartment.... So lady, if I don't give money to them, why should I give to any to you?"

...

Your mother, that fat domineering woman that has been living with us for the past 12 years, she has to go. "My God," my wife said, "I thought she was your mother."

...

One day I was telling the patient about the surgery she was about to undergo. I told her it was very risky. 99 out of 100 patients die. But the good thing, the last 99 I did had died.

...

People often ask me how have you made your marriage last so long. I told them, "We have a boxing match every Wednesday night." Last week the police wanted to know if I wanted to press charges.

...

I went to the doctor to be treated for pneumonia. He gave me so much penicillin, I sneezed and cured three patients.

...

If it weren't for Venetian blinds, it would be curtains for all of us.

...

Old Uncle Beduch entered his "Little Willie" in the Wounded Warrior program.

...

I could tell my wife was sick recently. The dishes were piling up in the sink.

...

I recently presented my comedy routine to one of the senior centers and I told my wife that I was a little nervous. She said "Don't worry nobody will laugh at you."

...

The patient of mine was quite upset and told me that he thought his wife was trying to poison him. I told him, "Let me talk to your wife and I will get back to you." The man came to see me next week and asked me if I had talked to his wife and I said, "Yes I have, take the poison."

...

If I knew the difference between antidote and anecdote, I could have saved a life instead of telling a funny story.

...

I went to the opera the other night and the woman sitting in front of me was blabbering away on her cell phone. She was very annoying, so I said, "Lady I can't hear." She turned around and said, "Sir, I wasn't talking to you."

...

Another thing helpful to our marriage is to go out every weekend for cocktails, dinner and dancing. She goes Friday and I go Saturday. (Henny Youngman)

...

I treated a giraffe for sore throat in the office last week, and it took me all day.

...

Last night at the restaurant we ordered a salad and the waiter asked "What kind of a dressing would I like?" I told him, "I would like a Russian dressing" They sent me a picture of Putin putting on his underpants.

...

Remember that saltpeter they gave us during the Vietnam war? It was used to keep us from chasing the women. I think it's starting to cut in.

...

The Dixieland band that I play in recently cut a CD. It sounds pretty good to me. The state of New York now uses it as a form of capital punishment.

...

It seems that my snoring is quite annoying, so my wife and I sleep in separate bedrooms. She sleeps in the main bedroom and makes me sleep in Tucson.

...

It seems like everything has a drive-in-service nowadays. Even our funeral director has a drive-in called Jump-in the-Box.

...

I told my wife, "I thought our children were spoiled." She didn't think so. She thought they just smelled that way.

...

I saw a movie actress. She had so much silicone in her breasts she could caulk a bathtub.

...

I went to a restaurant the other night I had been some time ago. I said to the waitress, "It's been 10 years since I've been here." She said " Don't blame me, I'm working as fast as I can."

...

One evening we were performing Dixieland band music and someone asked me "How late does the band play?" I said, "About a half a beat behind the drummer."

...

New breakfast cereals have so much fiber they come with their own roll of toilet paper.

...

At this supermarket the other day, I saw a man pushing about 20 shopping carts. I said, "Don't hog all of the carts, maybe somebody else would like one."

...

Beduch hates sex in the movies. He tried it once, the seat folded up and he spilled his coffee.

...

A buddy of mine was having trouble with his health insurance. I guess they said "moron" was a pre-existing disease.

...

My wife loves to shop. She was sick for a week and three stores went under at Crossgates Mall.

...

Donna lost her credit card but I didn't report it because whoever found it is spending less.

...

I didn't realize that my Uncle Beduch drank so much until he showed up sober one day.

...

One of the men at work had such bad body odor he used industrial strength Raid as a deodorant.

...

Someone asked me how Beduch broke his arm and I told them, "He bought a book on the *Joy of Sex* and there was a misprint on page 279."

...

We have a nice dog and my wife told me that the dog needed to be fed. I told her, "No he doesn't, I can smell the mailman on his breath."

...

Beduch hates sex in the movies. He tried it once, the seat folded up and he spilled his coffee.

...

I was having lunch with a thrice-married friend and I said to him, "Ralph did you ever say anything to your wife you were sorry you said? He thought for a few moments and said, "*I do* comes to mind."

...

I was married by a judge. I should've asked for a jury.

...

The waitress asked me what kind a salad I would like? I said "I would like to have the chef's salad, but then what would the chef eat?"

...

You marry the man of your dreams and 14 years later you are married to a couch that burps.

...

I'm pushing 80, I figure that's enough exercise for the day.

...

My dad named me after a town in Massachusetts. It's called Marblehead.

...

My wife said I'm nosy. At least that's what her diary said.

...

My buddy and I were playing in the swing band and I asked, "Did you hear my last solo?" He said, "I certainly hope so."

...

Victoria's Secret is that nobody older than 20 can fit into their stuff.

...

One of the great mysteries of life is how a 2-pound box of chocolates can put 5 pounds on a woman.

...

The economy is so bad Pfizer pharmaceuticals had to lay off two Congressmen and a Senator.

...

I always hold my wife's hand wherever we go. I'm afraid she'll hit me.

. . .

The bride was so ugly we had a throw a bone down the aisle to get her to move.

. . .

I went to the doctors the other day and I got a bill for $250. I sent a check and added a note and said for those prices, I would think you could put out some wine and cheese.

. . .

"Angelina Jolie doesn't do anything for me," I told my wife. And she said, "Nobody could do anything for you."

. . .

I finally figured out what women want. They want security. Every time I talk to one, they yell *Security*!

. . .

First chair on the trumpet, captain of the football team, valedictorian of the class -- not bad for being homeschooled.

. . .

Imagine Mary telling Joseph that she was pregnant. The first words were probably, "Jesus Christ!" Mary said, "What a great name if it's a boy!"

. . .

How did your husband die? Did he die laughing or was he tickled to death?

. . .

I used to date a pretty large woman. When we walked on the beach people would ask me what I used for bait. (Rodney Dangerfield)

...

An old man married a young girl and was reciting his vows to the preacher. He didn't say "I do," but "I'll try."

...

My buddy is so old he embarrassed everybody by asking for seconds at the Last Supper.

...

When Dean Martin performed, women used to throw their hotel keys at him. When I perform women still throw their keys, but it's after they have left the room.

...

When my daughter was pregnant, I was so excited. I didn't know whether I would be a grandfather or grandmother.

...

Many people are joining a gym. My nephew gets his exercise running from the cops.

...

Have you met my wife Donna? Yes you have? Would you like to meet her again?

...

Adam said to Eve "What do you mean you don't have anything to wear?" (Red Buttons)

...

Are you frustrated trying to get the tops off of your child-proof medicines? A friend of mine damn near had heart attack trying to get the top off his nitroglycerin bottle.

...

Gosh, even fertilizer bags have their tops stitched with heavy string. What are they protecting Romanoff jewels?

...

At Proctors recently, the stage manager opened the curtain to say the show was canceled because the lead actor had died. From the balcony a lady yelled, "Give him an enema." The manager yelled back "That won't help." and the lady replied , "It won't hurt."

...

I'm a tired old man and I should be home on in bed alone. In all these years watching television, I never stayed awake for the late show and recently fell asleep for the early show. I can hardly keep my eyes open for the news at noon. (Abe Vigoda)

...

Kane's wife divorced him because he wasn't Abel. (Red Buttons)

...

My wife suggested we renew our marriage vows. I told her, "I didn't know they expired."

...

Song: *I hurt my knee falling for you.*

...

A patient asked my wife what kind of doctor I was? "Only fair" she said.

...

Woody Allen says, "The thing he likes about sex is it doesn't require special shoes."

...

No matter how good she looks, there is some man that is tired of putting up with her BS.

...

They tell me marriage is a partnership. I guess I'm the silent partner.

...

Dad was a lawyer, Mom was a heart surgeon and my sister a nuclear engineer. Me, I like to color.

...

Famous Quotes: Lot's mother said to Lot when his wife was turned into a pillar of salt, "Salt we got plenty, what we need is coffee."

...

Washington said as he was crossing the Delaware, "Everybody's going to Miami and I'm going to Trenton."

...

Christopher Columbus said to Queen Isabella, "The world is round, you're the one that's flat."

...

Julius Caesar said to Brutus when he was being stabbed, "You know this blows the Christmas bonus."

...

Goliath's mother said to Goliath "Stop hanging around with David, you're always coming home stoned."

...

Jack the Ripper's mother said to him "How come I never see you with the same woman?"

...

Adam said to the Lord, "What's for dinner, ribs again?" (Thank you, Red Buttons, for those)

...

The audiologist was checking my hearing the other day. In the booth, they played a Christmas carol: *Do You Hear What I Hear?*

...

The organ donation program set up by New York State has a theme song: *I Only Have Eyes for You.*

...

A police officer was asked what would you do if you had to arrest your mother-in-law. He said, "I call for backup."

...

Do I like rap music? I often listen to it in the car. It is usually from a car 10 vehicles in front of me.

...

Sydney Goldberg's favorite good luck charm is a rabbi's foot.

...

Donald Trump has quite an ego. He is at the Vatican's Sistine Chapel having a fresco painted of himself.

...

Sex, the most fun I ever had without laughing. (Woody Allen)

...

I saw my doctor today because I was having trouble with my pacemaker. Every time I farted the garage door would open.

...

If I had a head that looked like yours, I would have it circumcised.

...

My friend wanted to buy a year's supply of prophylactics, but the drugstore wouldn't just sell him one.

...

My wife cooked a three-bean chili. It gave me so much gas I am being followed by three Saudi Secret Service agents

...

A buddy knew he was in trouble when his ex-wife turned out to be his blind date.

...

Amelia Earhart said, "Stop looking for me and find my luggage." (Red Buttons)

...

A peeping Tom threw up outside my window. (Rodney Dangerfield)

...

Was it Donald Trump that said to the Pope after lunch, "Next time bring the little woman."

...

After a particularly boring political speech, where the Senator was calling for land reform, school reform and political reform, Uncle Beduch sitting in the audience yelled CHLOROFORM.

...

Beduch was an interesting guy. He always said he had a trophy wife. What he didn't tell you was that it was the trophy for last place. But she did get 251 get-well cards.

...

I went to bad Mexican restaurant and asked, "What's the catch of the day?" "Hepatitis!" they said.

...

When you get old, you lose the hair on the top of your head and seems like the only places it grows is in your ears and nose. I now go to the barber so I can hear and breath.

...

A lady friend told me she was on the pill. "Which one, Nitroglycerin?"

...

Uncle Beduch's first wife was so big the Post Office gave her own zip code.

...

My daughter told me her dog just delivered a litter of puppies, "The way she shakes her ass, I'm not surprised," I said.

...

My wife is half Jewish and half Irish, all her life she wants to buy liquor at wholesale prices.

...

Uncle Beduch has been having trouble with his vision. He told me the doctor said he had a detached rectum.

...

Life is like a roll of toilet paper. The closer to the end, the faster it goes.

...

This is the IRS calling Rabbi Silver. "Did a Mr. Sanford Weinstein donate ten thousand dollars to your congregation?" "No, but he will." Rabbi Silver replied.

...

Beduch looks like the calf that just found out where veal comes from.

...

Grandchildren are great, but just how long can you say the pig goes oink and the cow says moo. I feel like I'm talking to a supermodel. (Joan Rivers)

...

Nice thing about being so old is you don't get calls anymore from life insurance salesmen.

...

"Long time no see," I said to my ophthalmologist.

...

I asked my wife, "What are those little blue and white flowers in her garden, I forgot their names?" She said "They are called forget-me-nots."

...

My wife and I live in Holy Acrimony.

...

Beduch's wife is so old her G String is now a Bb.

...

MOSTLY ONE LINERS CAUSE I CAN'T REMEMBER TWO...

Old Beduch slept like a baby last night. He woke up 3 AM crying with a load in his pants.

...

My old car went for an oil change at Jiffy Lube today. The mechanic looked at it and told me "Keep the oil, change the car."

...

Donna told me that the only thing I can turn on at my age is the electric blanket.

...

When she didn't want any more children, my niece had a IED placed, I figured that would take care things permanently. I can't wait until the bomb defecates.

...

The bank asked if I wanted them to check my balance. I said yes, so they pushed me over.

...

I was so depressed about the election, I called the suicide hot line and they connected me to a man in Syria. He asked me if I could drive a truck.

...

I asked Beduch where he got a black eye. He said, "A young girl had a T shirt on that said *Guess* and he responded *implants* and she decked him."

...

Historians can study at the Bush Library, Carter Library, Reagan Library, and also the Bill Clinton adult bookstore. I hear he is signing Monica's new book.

...

My very old car has trouble at night. I think the mechanic said the headlights have cataracts. I had a bifocal windshield inserted. When I get registered now, they give me upper and lower plates.

...

My college roommate called me and told me he upped his pledge to Georgetown University and asked me to do the same. I told him, "Up yours."

...

At a funeral for a man that drown, I told the widow "I heard he left you over a million dollars. Pretty good for a man that couldn't read or write." "Well, he couldn't swim either" she said.

...

I am quite proud of my grandson. He won trustee of the month at Sing Sing for September.

...

For a heckler: "Is it time for your medicine or too much coffee this morning?"

...

Song: *It's hard to kiss the lips at night that chew out my ass all day long.* (Vince Gill)

...

United Airlines has a new regulation for carry-on baggage. It must be able to be stored in the butt crack of the passenger in front of you.

...

Song: *Looking for a 10 in a Motel 6*. Now they changed its name to the *Quick Sheet Motel.*

...

At Beduch's age, he still chases women, but only down hill.

...

Beduch told me he likes shopping at Dollar General. You don't have to get all dressed up like you do when you go to Walmart.

...

The drummer in our swing band can't be beat. But maybe he should be.

...

"I love you darling." Then Donna asks "Is that you or the beer talkin?" "Talkin' to the beer, Hon!"

...

Quits, strange name for a boy? Well Dad said, "If its a girl call it Lilah, if it is boy we'll call it Quits."

...

A young intern asked me, "How do I get to the ICU?" "Well, first you have to be very sick." I said.

...

Do you know what time it is? I'm sorry I'm not from around here. (Steven Wright)

...

General George Custer was the first man to wear an arrow shirt.

...

Yes, I think you've lost some weight. Your double chin does look smaller.

...

A man walks into a bar and says to the bartender "give me a double bourbon." So the bartender says, "You seem upset" and the man said, "Yes I am, my son just told me he's gay." "I'll also buy you a bourbon." A week later the man comes in again and this time orders a triple bourbon. "What's wrong?" "My other son just told me he is gay." Surprised, the bartender says, "Doesn't anyone like women in your family?" "Yes, my wife."

...

On my new program to lose weight, I've been ordering diet water.

...

Would you care to donate anything to the Southwest Indian Relief Fund, Mrs. Custer?

...

I have been learning Spanish by calling the bank and pressing button number two.

...

How am I expected to get this gadget to work if half the directions are in Spanish?

...

When my doctor friend got married again, all the motels in the area flew their sheets at half-mast. Also they had a memorial service and then entered his zipper in the hall of fame.

...

A friend of mine married a 7-foot woman. His friends put him up to it.

...

I worked with a nurse who could make the patient without disturbing the bed.

...

What really upsets Beduch is his 13-year-old granddaughter smoking in front of her three children.

...

When my wife gives me the silent treatment, she thinks that's punishment.

...

She said, "How can you leave in the middle of the conversation?" I said, "That's only the middle?"

...

My Grandson weighed 6 pounds at birth. After he was circumcised, only 4.

...

Today a marriage is called successful if it outlasts the milk.

...

I'm really proud of my gold watch. My grandfather sold it to me on his deathbed.

...

Beduch took his wife to a wife swapping party. He didn't make out well. He had to throw in some cash.

...

Beduch went to reform school on a scholarship.

...

He made a killing on Wall Street. He shot his broker.

...

You can easily judge the character of the man by how he treats those that can do nothing for him.

...

Grandpa Spring spent all his money on booze and broads. The rest he wasted.

. . .

Donna and I often walk arm and arm, not because of love, but to hold each other up.

. . .

My first date said, "I'd love to kiss you, but I just washed my hair." (Betty Davis)

. . .

When my daughter didn't know what to name her twins, her cousin suggested Denise and Da-nephew. I suggested Pete and Repeat?"

. . .

At a Chinese restaurant last week the waitress asked me if I wanted Won Ton soup. "No, I replied, how about Two Ton soup?"

. . .

Egg Tu Yung is a Chinese word for premature baby.

. . .

My grandson got a job for the summer working as a lifeguard in the car wash.

. . .

I saw a man walking out of Walmart with 100 rolls of toilet paper. I said to him, "Gosh, if you're having a problem you really should see a doctor."

. . .

"Your call is important to us. Please wait, you are currently number 1230 and the wait times are approximately seven months. My colleague in New Delhi currently is studying English in a technical support group and should return shortly."

...

Scientists have discovered that man can be in the frozen state of suspended animation for up to five years and not lose his job at the Post Office.

...

When I was in high school, I might be considered an honor student. Seems all I could say was, "Yes, your Honor, no, your Honor."

...

Grandson Johnny is the teacher's pet. She can't afford a dog.

...

I'd kill for a Nobel Peace Prize.

...

Now that I've learned to make the most of life, most of it is gone.

...

Son-in-law Mike went hunting with two Italians from New Jersey. They went on a bear hunt and found four bears floating face down, with their hands tied behind their backs in the Hudson river.

...

The grade school I went to as a kid was so tough we had our own coroner. If we weren't home by 11 o'clock, we would be declared legally dead. I could walk 30 minutes and never leave the scene of the crime. The most common means of transportation was the police car.

...

I saw a great heavyweight fight the other night. Two women at a Chinese buffet were fighting over a glazed ham.

...

Beduch has been dating an anorexic girl but he is seeing less and less of her.

...

My wife loves to shop at Dollar General. She usually puts everything on layaway.

...

As you get older your hearing starts to go. Now most of the conversation between my wife and myself consists of, "What, I can't hear you, the oven is on."

...

I don't remember my wife's birthday, but I do know she was born at a very young age.

...

Don't kiss me, I've got a lip fungus that hasn't been identified yet.

...

Please wake Jack up and turn on his pacemaker. Tell him I am delighted his widow could be here tonight.

...

I didn't like my beard at first. But it kind of grew on me.

...

I used to date a stripper called Ginger -- Ginger Vitus. She had a great body but lousy teeth.

...

Uncle Beduch doesn't object to same-sex marriages. He's been married 50 years and the sex is the same all the time.

...

The last time our band played we got a standing ovation. The audience stood up and walked out.

...

My son-in-law got me camouflage toilet seat. It gives me an excuse when I miss.

...

Lincoln's Gettysburg address was 230 words. I wonder how he remembered his address and did he get any mail there?

...

Obesity is a problem in the Navy. One of the officers is so big he is called the Big Rear Admiral.

...

Have you ever been convicted of a felony? No, but my hearing is next week.

...

I received a request for a recommendation for a job from an old friend. So I wrote, "I knew him well, we were roommates in prison."

...

When we're young we always seem to have a crush on our teachers. For me it was my wife's aerobic instructor.

...

Old Beduch said he doesn't talk during sex. He doesn't want to wake his wife. (Rodney Dangerfield)

...

When my wife needed some feminine protection, I went and brought home an AR 15.

...

Once I dated a very classy girl. When she passed gas, she covered her mouth. (Rodney Dangerfield)

...

The doctor told my mother when I was born, we did everything we could but I pulled through anyway. (Henny Youngman)

...

The doctor was so angry after I was born, he slapped the stork. (Rodney Dangerfield)

...

The clerk was cashing a check for a lady and she asked the woman for a street name on the check. The young woman said she didn't have a street name, but that you could call her Juanita.

...

Uncle Beduch got a ticket the other day for DWI -- Driving While Incontinent.

...

Poor Uncle Beduch went to the doctor the other day and told him that he thought his wife had VD. The doctor quickly gave himself a shot of penicillin.

...

My partner's son recently married a young lady from Beijing. He told me how wonderful the wedding reception was. I asked "What did you do for the food, send out for Chinese?"(Not funny, he told me.)

...

Abraham Lincoln on his deathbed said to his wife, "You and your Goddamn theater parties."

...

I say this from the bottom of my heart, "You are not a well man. You need care and help. You dribble all over yourself and frequently wet your pants." (Don Rickles)

...

Guys in our band would rather work in New York rather than California because they get paid three hours earlier.

. . .

When I asked the waitress how long a wait for the table, she told me 45 minutes. " I am almost 80, I don't know if I have that long."

. . .

Did I tell you when my daughter delivered the twins, the water broke and the dog drown.

. . .

Never did I believe my prostate would be bigger than my ego.

. . .

When I was a young boy I was so ugly that when I went by a toilet it flushed.

. . .

The terrorists captured all the accordion players in Iraq. They threatened to release one an hour until their demands were met. Talk about terror.

. . .

Recently Beduch buried his mother-in-law. I guess he should've waited till she died.

. . .

Uncle Ralph has so much gas that his wife won't get into the car unless she puts a canary in first.

. . .

A friend of mine gave a piano recital. It wasn't very good. Steinway personally rubbed his name off the instrument.

. . .

In the elevator there were two gorgeous women and an old man. One lady takes out her perfume and sprays her neck and says "Ralph Lauren, hundred and fifty an ounce." The next woman sprays her neck and announces, "Chanel Number Five, $200 an ounce." The door opens and the old man leaves and as he goes, he lets out with the terrible fart. He turns and says, "Broccoli $.49 a pound"

. . .

Jack, the last person that thought you were funny, died in the Glendale nursing home last week.

. . .

When a guest at your party stays to long, try this line. "Come again when you can't stay so long."

. . .

"Make yourself comfortable and hit somebody, Frank." (Don Rickles)

. . .

I heard the Pope said that when he retired, he wanted to spend more time with his wife and children.

. . .

Moses said, as he came down from Mount Sinai, "The food in this hospital is terrible, put me back on IV's." (Red Buttons)

. . .

MOSTLY ONE LINERS CAUSE I CAN'T REMEMBER TWO...

Orville Wright said to his brother, "We are in the air 12 minutes and our luggage ends up in Cleveland."

. . .

The Hunchback of Notre Dame said to his tailor Irving, "Work a little more on the coat, slacks are fine."

. . .

"Who dresses you -- Stevie Wonder?" (Don Rickles)

. . .

We are talking old. That person has an autographed copy of the Bible.

. . .

Two Jewish women were having lunch and the waitress came by and asked, "Is ANYTHING is OK?"

. . .

I'm not sure there is an afterlife but I'm going to bring a change of underwear just in case. (Woody Allen)

. . .

They married late in life. It's so sweet, they have a matching pair of Med -Alert bracelets.

. . .

Black is a great color for you. It matches your eyes.

. . .

I'll never forget your last performance. But I'll certainly give it a try.

. . .

If you are worried about somebody sitting next to you on the airplane. You can wear a T-shirt that says "Let me tell you about Jesus."

. . .

She has spent more time on her back then Michelangelo did painting the ceiling in the Sistine Chapel.

. . .

The more you say the less people remember.

. . .

When you're talking about someone you don't care for and he tells you that he's been sick. If you've got the temerity, you can say "I hope it's something serious."

. . .

His wife really pampers him and when they're on sale she will use Depends.

. . .

There is a diaper changing station in the men's room at the Mohawk Golf Club and it's not for babies.

...

That man's pretty old. He was a waiter at the Last Supper.

...

I played a gig and the drummer asked, "When was the last time we played together Doc?"...TONIGHT!

...

Stick around for the fight, we are not going to pay the band.

...

Brunhilde, the nurse with the Nazi unibrow and the iron cross on her cap, received flowers for the patient. She asked if she should unwrap them now or save them for the funeral?

...

My daughter adopted a timid pit bull. He bites his nails.

...

I had a patient that broke her ankle and I asked, "How that happen?" " In the glove compartment of my boyfriend's car," she said.

...

Neighbors adopted a little baby girl from China. They are learning Mandarin so when she starts to talk they can understand her.

...

He's a complete stranger and not even a close one at that. (Groucho)

...

The slacks I bought at the Salvation Army were a little long. I had to unzip the fly to blow my nose.

...

The sound of that man's voice is so boring I can't believe he doesn't put himself to sleep.

...

A Negro man walked into a southern restaurant and the waiter said, "We don't serve blacks here." He said, "It's OK, I don't eat them."

...

Sign in men's room in Syria: In case of drone attack, hide under the urinal; it hasn't been hit since World War II.

...

Another sign in the men's room over the urinal that said "If you are having trouble voiding, call Doctor Rosenbaum." He's my urologist!

...

The police arrested a transvestite for male fraud!

...

My wife said, when I got home late one night, "Your eyes look glazed." " I stopped at Dunkin' Donuts on the way home, sweetheart."

...

Seems like I'm getting forgetful. I walked into a bar last night and said, "Do I come here often?"

...

Uncle Beduch was so ugly he planned to donate his face to the National Wildlife Bureau. (Ali)

...

Jogging is for people not intelligent to watch television.

...

A 737 United airplane crashed in the cemetery. Recovery workers have found 3251 bodies so far.

...

You only live once and that's probably enough.

...

We came from pretty poor family. I used wear hand-me-down clothes. The problem was I had three sisters.

...

Ever notice when you're over the hill you seem to pick up speed?

...

Mom wanted me to be a priest, but I couldn't drink that early in the morning.

...

The town we lived in was so poor that the pawn shop sign only had one ball.

...

How old are you, 81? You certainly look every day of it.

...

You look very young, you still have pimples.

...

While walking by a cemetery one day, two guys started chasing me with shovels. (Rodney Dangerfield)

...

The closest to 4.0 I ever got in college was my blood-alcohol level.

...

I think your gene pool could use a little more chlorine.

...

Some mornings I wake up grumpy and other mornings I let her sleep.

...

That person is a born pessimist. When he smells flowers he looks for the coffin. Even his blood type is B negative.

...

Beduch has been on so many blind dates that the Association of the Blind gave him a free dog.

...

I had amnesia once, I don't know, maybe it was twice.

...

Republicans and Democrats finally agree on one thing. Raise their salaries.

...

Anna Phylactic and her younger brother Prophylactic.

...

Don't forget, it is time to wet your plants.

...

A court of law is like a bagpipe solo. You can't wait till the case is closed.

...

Donald Trump is a fast talker and could sell aluminum siding to the owner of a brickhouse.

...

He is the kind of a man that would throw a beer party and lock the bathroom door.

...

Crime is down in Schenectady. They ran out of victims.

...

I was at Georgetown University for two terms: Woodrow Wilson and Warren Harding.

...

I'm telling you, he is such a big person that the bathtub has stretch marks and the water rises in the toilets when he bathes.

...

When the lights dim at a diner, I say, "I guess they just electrocuted the chef."

...

Business was so bad last year. I got a get-well card from the IRS.

...

One nephew is a small kid. When he was born his father passed out cigar butts.

...

The other nephew is tall. He's got a job cleaning giraffe ears at the zoo.

...

That man's been married so many times he's got rice burns.

...

He is so big I think he was born on June 6 -7- 8.

...

My doctor told me, "Drink lemon juice after a hot bath." It was for my sore throat. I could never finish drinking hot bath.

...

All the lies about him are true.

...

I'm sure when your ship comes in, there will be a dock strike.

...

He is the ultimate laxative.

...

You can observe a lot just by watching. (Yogi)

...

Most of the future lies ahead. (Yogi)

...

My wife said that she saw Dr..Zhivago. I said to her, "What's wrong with you now?"

...

My body moves so slowly they track me with the sundial.

...

We were a poor family. When I threw the dog a bone, it would have to call fair catch.

...

Our band likes to play at the prisons because nobody can walk out during the show.

...

Once I worked for a fire hydrant factory, but I couldn't park anywhere near the place. (Steven Wright)

...

I got bitten by a tiny little bug and I didn't even see him. I asked my wife what they called. NO-SEE-UUMS.

...

I knew when it was time to retire from surgery. When I completed a surgery, my wife was in the recovery room booing me.

...

I came from a small town. Its primary industry was returning beer bottles back to the store. The telephone directory is one page, the town prostitute was a virgin and the first baby of the year born in July.

...

Beduch's wife talked to him briefly on the phone for an hour and a half.

...

Don't forget to include plenty of money for sympathy cards in your retirement planning. Jez! I wonder if I can buy them in bulk at Costco.

...

It was so wet and muddy this spring, I saw my neighbor planting rice.

...

If Americans throw rice at the wedding, do the Chinese throw hotdogs?

...

It was so hot this summer, I saw a dog chasing a cat. They were both walking.

...

My new diet works so well, McDonald's and Wendy's are suing me for nonsupport.

...

My brother asked the nursing home activities director if he could play the accordion for the residents. The director said, "How about $50?" Paul said, "Great, most people charge me $75."

...

For sale by owner: *Wedding dress, slightly used only four times, I've given up hope.*

...

Jack is my best friend. It gives you some idea how difficult it is for me to make friends.

...

How do you like my new sport coat? My wife got it for me. When I came home early one afternoon, I found it hanging over the bedroom chair.

...

My cousin said to his wife, "When you married me it was like you won the New York State lottery," and she said "What, the dollar scratch off?"

...

The snake escaped from the zoo last week and I think they called it A Reptile Dysfunction, or RD.

...

When I was young all I wanted was a BMW. Now I would settle for two thirds of that.... a BM.

...

When my wife looked into the mirror she wasn't happy with what she saw. I said, "Don't worry honey, it's an old mirror."

...

When we played the nursing home with the band, a grumpy old lady yelled "you're too loud!" I yelled back, "Turn down your hearing aid!"

...

The roofer asked if I want a 30 year or 40 year shingle? "I need something that lasts about 2 years."

...

The Cleveland Clinic cardiology and surgery department has hired a new spokesman, Bob Newhart.

...

Good to see you. When did you get out?

...

Beduch gave his wife flowers for her birthday.
So she said to her friend, "I suppose I'll have to spend the weekend with my legs up in the air." "My goodness, don't you have a vase?" she responded.

...

My married friend visited a lady of the evening and she asked, "Need a receipt?"

...

I believe in the hereafter. I often walk in a room and say "What am I here after?"

...

There was a universally disliked man that had died and during his eulogy the pastor asked if someone could say something nice about the deceased. After a long period of silence, a voice from the back the room finally yelled "his brother was worse."

...

At a cocktail party one of the woman said "I have never been so insulted my life" and I said, "Stick around, it's early in the night." (Groucho)

...

When the trombone player hits that high note usually all my plants die.

...

As we get older the house is too big and the medicine cabinet is too small.

...

Roses are reddish, violets are bluish, if it weren't for Jesus, we'd all be Jewish.

...

We went to my daughter's house for dinner. She was serving lamb and I told her "I didn't like lamb." She replied, "Mary had a Little Lamb."

...

I'm always a sucker for a girl with a mustache.

...

Some time ago I went to an antique auction with my wife. Believe it or not, there were three people that bid on me. If it had been another $50 my wife would've sold me.

...

Age is not important unless you're cheese.

...

My patient's breath was so bad, I didn't know whether to offer him mint or a roll of toilet paper.

...

Beduch belched and killed all the birds in the backyard.

...

Who put that brush next to the toilet? That damn thing hurts like hell!

...

When the band plays, the most frequent request is how to get to the restroom.

...

I think my doctor is losing it. He grabbed my knee, told me to cough and then hit me in the balls with a hammer.

...

That man is not exactly an underwear model.

...

My doctor said something that worried me. He told me that they were going to name a disease after me.

...

I'm not doing very well in the stock market. My broker has me invested in the Stunted Growth Fund, the Poor Value Line Commodities, and Detroit municipal bonds. He works for the Infidelity and No Trust Group. I think it is part of Bernie Madoff's outfit. Bernie has *made off* with a lot of my money.

...

You know how to get a woman to say yes? Ask her if you are bothering her?

...

At my age, a nice way to see all your friends is to visit the cemetery.

...

Most of the Dixieland band records are at the police station.

...

I asked the midget for a loan and he said, "I can't now, I'm a little short."

...

Uncle Beduch's wife is a so bad a cook they don't brush their teeth after a meal, they count them. They pray after they eat. The garbage disposal even threw up and the cockroaches hung themselves.

...

My mother-in-law is suing McDonald's because her coffee fell in her lap and it froze.

...

Calling you stupid is an insult to stupid people.

. . .

Jewish parents often put a lot of pressure on their children to get good marks. I saw one bumper sticker that said, "If my son had just studied a little harder, he too, would've been an honor student at Burnt Hills High School."

. . .

The police are toughening up their sobriety tests. Not only do you have to blow up a balloon, now you have to twist it into a giraffe.

. . .

George Bush reads the Bible every day. You would think by his age he would've finished by now.

. . .

I think I'm confused. I scratched my watch and wound up my ass.

. . .

Tucson, Arizona has so many cacti they had to change the county seat three times.

. . .

It was raining cats and dogs. Daughter Lisa found a great, but wet, puppy under a tree.

. . .

A lot of the guys in the Dixie band have difficulty reading music. The banjo player even has trouble reading.

. . .

That man's house is so big, he has three ZIP Codes and a gift store on the second floor.

. . .

If girls want to wear short shorts, I'm behind them all the way.

. . .

The recently released movie on the Iraq War made 35 million dollars. One million on the movie and 34 million on the popcorn.

. . .

Never accept a drink from a urologist.

. . .

The airplane take off was a little hairy. The hostess asked what I would like to drink. "I'll take whatever the pilot is drinking!"

...

At the end of the night, my wife could hardly keep her mouth open.

...

There was an ad in the newspaper for a grave marker: *Second-hand tombstone for sale. Great buy for a person named Murphy.*

...

My wife said my trumpet playing isn't as bad as it sounds. (Donna)

...

Now that I am retired, the only way I can tell the day of the week is that on Sunday the *New York Times* is really big and you can get hurt if it falls on you.

...

When age crawls up on us, it takes twice as long to look half as good.

...

With a urine output of 100cc/day and on renal dialysis, my brother said, "Look on the bright side, at least you don't have to get up in the middle of the night to go to the bathroom."

...

Man, you're like a toenail fungus, I can't get rid of you.

...

And now a word from our sponsor Alka Selzer......
Burp!

...

A older couple in the office were recently married, he was 92 and his wife 89. They are registered at CVS pharmacy and Medicare is paying the hospital for their honeymoon.

...

I had been taking trumpet lessons but had trouble with my teachers: Some have quit, some suggest I try bass drum, others ask how can I stand it. And still others have turned to drugs and alcohol.

...

We had a cured ham for the holidays. I wonder what disease it had?

...

My partner's daughter got married and they were registered at Crate and Barrel. It's strange I never got a thank you note. I got her a crate, maybe she wanted a barrel.

...

Police found the body of a nurse washed up on the Mohawk River. They identified it as a nurse because her stomach was empty, her bladder full and her ass had been chewed out.

...

Beduch's wife is a great driver. She is so good she can drive from the back seat.

...

My conductor yelled, "Jack, I can't hear the 4th trumpet." "Who cares, anyone listening?

...

Once I lost a hundred pounds and my wife said "Yes, I can see it in your face."

...

Beduch's career was unblemished by lack of significant achievement.

...

My cousin Louie goes to the first Deformed Lutheran Church, my wife and I go to Immaculate Deception Catholic Church and my daughters go to Our Lady of Perpetual Payments. When the children were small they went to our Sisters of No Mercy religious school.

...

There is so much smog in Tucson the street signs are in braille.

...

They have cards for every occasion, Mother's Day, Father's Day, etc. I went into Hallmark's and asked if they had a "humorous sympathy section" and do you have a "controlling bitch section" for my buddy?

...

Many seniors retire to the state of Florida. The leading industry is a funeral business.

...

The Jewish faith bury their deceased quickly. Uncle Melvin, who suffers from narcolepsy, has already been buried five times.

...

It was a long boring speech. I needed a shave when it was over.

...

Oh, I couldn't eat dessert, thank you. I won't have enough room for my pills.

...

My grandson got a great job. He is working for GM this summer as a crash test dummy.

...

For our anniversary this year we had a candlelight dinner at our house. The storm took the power out.

...

He's not a bad guy, that is until you get to know him.

...

I went to a funeral recently in the Catholic Church and told my wife I hadn't been in the church in a long time. I said "What do I do next?" "Pray for forgiveness." she said. (Donna)

...

I was listening to a recording of my favorite trumpet player, Harry James, play *Stardust*. He makes the same damn mistake every time I listen to that recording. You would think by now he could get it right.

...

As a teenager I was a 90 lb. weakling. Now at almost 80, I'm a 190 lb. weakling!

...

While performing the stand up routine at Glendale Nursing Home I asked the director, "How much time do I have?" She yelled back, "Stay up there until you get a laugh."

...

I saw a sign that said WET FLOOR, and I did and got arrested.

...

Everybody going to the gym to be healthy will end up in the hospital dying of nothing.

...

At my age, I never buy the extended warranty.

...

After Uncle Beduch had been married 25 years, he called his father-in-law to find out if there were a return policy with the marriage contract.

...

It gets tougher and tougher at the gym. It's an effort to put on my gym clothes. I asked the trainer, "Could that be counted as part of my workout and how about running late?"

...

Uncle Beduch went to the eye doctor and said, "I need my eyes examined." "You sure do buddy, this is the ladies room."

...

I was trying my on old uniform from Vietnam and I'm proud to tell you the socks and tie still fit.

...

Currently, I'm taking so many pills Bristol Myers Squibb had to put on a second shift.

...

When good old Uncle Beduch was a younger man he had a date with a prostitute. "Not on the first date," she said. (Rodney Dangerfield)

...

The bagpipes are so strident that I'm going to have them play at my funeral. I want folks to know there is something worse than death. You know, maybe a little oil on that thing would help.

...

I've been in medicine a long time. I was the chief medical officer on Noah's Arc and even did the circumcision on Hippocrates.

...

When we are on a gig, I protect my trumpet by hiding it in an accordion case.

...

Old Beduch says he wants to drown his troubles but he can't get his wife to go swimming.

...

My wife wanted to go some place for our anniversary that she hasn't been. I suggested the kitchen. (It wasn't a good night.)

...

Remember when it was easy to buy gas. Tell the attendant put in 10 bucks and you got your windshield washed. Nowadays, so many questions:
>
> *Do you have a EZ supermarket card?*
> *Pay inside or out?*
> *Want a receipt?*
> *Debit or Credit?*
> *PIN number?*
> *Insert your card swiftly...sorry not quick enough.*
> *Enter you Zip Code*
> *Select the grade of gas you want.*
> *Do you want a car wash?*
> *What color socks was last customer wearing?*

I ran out of gas before completing all the questions.

...

Rich would first to tell you he's a difficult man and I would be the second.

. . .

My grandson told me I was cool. I said "You don't look so hot yourself."

. . .

Ralph is a little conceited, he may die in his own arms.

. . .

A *wind driven pitch approximater*, that's a synonym for the trombone.

. . .

He's the kinda guy if you ask him how he is doing, he is stuck for an answer. (Lauren Bacall)

. . .

The restaurant has a diet Thousand Island salad dressing. It's called 500 Island.

. . .

The Jewish families often name their children for individuals from the First Testament. Well my friend's son is a Rabbi and they recently had a baby boy. I was asked "What do you think the boy was named?" I said "I dunno, maybe Christian?"

...

I arrived bright and early one day, well OK, maybe just early.

...

It would be great to live to be one hundred. Very few people die at a hundred.

...

We thank you from the heart of my bottom.

...

For a heckler: "It is surprising such a big head holds such a small brain."

...

If dumb were a crime you would get the electric chair.

...

Our good friends had a party and one of the snobbish couples told us of all of their world travels: French Riviera, Safari in Africa, Great Wall of China etc. Finally, they asked where had Donna and I had been. "We took a bus ride to Buffalo once!" I said. That stopped things.

...

Passwords on your computer don't offer any damn security. Only thing they offer is frustration for the user!

...

I broke my glasses last week. I was splashing on some toilet water and the damn lid fell and hit me in the head.

...

If I knew I was going to live this long, I would have taken better care of myself. (George Burns at 100)

...

A few weeks ago my 6-year old grandson and I went for a haircut. When we were done, Johnny didn't look very happy with his haircut. "What's wrong buddy?" "Gosh Bepa, I wanted one like yours, with a hole in the top."

...

Went to the doctor the other day because I was having a problem with my jaw from chewing too much gum. I asked him what was the best course of action. He suggested I start smoking.

...

I guess I gained more weight. When I got on the scale today it said please deposit another quarter.

...

Macy's is offering a new line of men's fragrances:
1. Eau de Toilet of Morning Breath
2. Perspiration by Harry Pitts
3. Scent of Sidney's Shorts by Sadie Schwartz

...

My nephew was recently appointed CEO of a high-tech company. He said to me, "Do you know **many** women I had to sleep with to get where I am?"

...

I have put some weight on recently. For my birthday my wife bought me a pair of Chris Christie designer jeans.

...

At the gym I see a lot of tattoos on both sexes. One gorilla, all inked up, told me he only needed his card punched one more time and he would get a free one at Huey's House of Tattoos.

...

I haven't spoken to my wife for three weeks. I didn't want to interrupt her.

...

Beduch asked the clerk where the cigarette lighters were. He said, "Locked up with the adult books."

...

Women always seem to complain about men passing gas. It seems the reason they don't pass as much gas is they can't keep their mouths closed long enough to build up the pressure.

...

Recently, I went to a wedding where the bride was so homely everyone wanted to kiss the groom.

...

Nice thing about dating a homeless woman is at the end of the night you can drop her off anywhere.

...

Last week I tried to write an Irish drinking song but couldn't get past the first four bars.

...

The piano was invented so the musicians have someplace to put their drinks.

...

I heard all the toilet seats were stolen in the Schenectady Police Department. The police are looking into it, but they have nothing to go on.

...

I know when it's a singer knocking at the front door. They don't have the right key and don't know when to come in.

...

They have all sorts of wines nowadays. They even have one especially for men. It is called Pinot Mor.

. . .

I bought a pair of shoes on line and they were a little small. I didn't need a shoehorn, I needed a whole brass section.

. . .

Beduch's first wife got fired for sleeping with the boss. She worked for the Vatican.

. . .

When I got in the elevator the other day, a woman remarked, "Someone's deodorant isn't working." "It isn't me," I said, "I'm not wearing any."

. . .

My buddy says he's got the perfect secretary. She types fast and runs slow.

. . .

Have that woman scrubbed and sent to my tent. (overheard in Saudi Arabia)

. . .

You know where virgin wool comes from? Ugly sheep.

. . .

I don't like ice fishing. It's too hard to get the boat in the water.

. . .

Alitalia Airlines is merging with General Motors. They'll call the new airline "Genitalia"

. . .

When I started working out at the wellness center, I had an impersonal trainer. We meet at the gym, we don't talk, she works out a while and then we go home.

. . .

I was in bad shape when I started. For strength training they started me with balloons. After that, I progressed to the "Refrigerator Lunge," then the "Microwave Push" and finally the "12-oz Can Lift." I'll be honest, my favorite machine was the vending machine.

. . .

Donna and I were having dinner on the outside patio, when it started to rain. It took us two hours to finish the soup.

. . .

My daughters gave me the new iPhone 8 for my birthday. It'll hold two thousand songs or one message from my wife.

. . .

My father initially thought I was studying to be an astronaut. The dean at Georgetown called him and told him I was taking up space.

. . .

By the bedside in the hotel I was staying, there were two printed notes. One said: For those with a drinking problem called this number. So I did and it was a liquor store. Then I tried the other number that was there. It was "Dial a Prayer," they told me to go to hell.

. . .

Some recommended short story reading:
1. Amelia Earhart's guide to the Pacific.
2. The Engineer's Fashion Guide
3. Table Manners for your Harley Rendezvous Banquet

...

The grandson uses a lot of mousse in his hair. When he went for a hair cut, the barber asked him if he wanted a cut or an oil change?

...

A sexy blonde came into the waiting room but there were no seats available. She went to a gentleman and asked him if she could have his seat because she was pregnant. "You don't look pregnant, how far along are you?" he said. "About 2 hours."

...

In the Schenectady High School English class, the teacher asked, "What comes after a sentence?" A tough looking kid in the front row said, "An appeal."

...

My compassionate partner wanted to open a half way house for girls that won't go all the way.

...

At a friend's divorce proceeding, the judge said he was going to give the ex-wife 3000 dollars a month. My buddy said, "Gee whiz judge, that's mighty generous of you, believe me I will try to throw in a little myself."

...

My cardiologist tells me to eat healthy things. Donna made a wonderful salad last night. It was composed of spinach, walnuts, tangerines, chicken and then smothered with pigeon milk. It was great, only problem was 10 minutes after eating it, I pooped on the windshield of my car.

...

An old timer was returning for a follow-up visit and I asked how he was doing? "Much better since I started the new medicine you gave me Doc, *End It All*. "End It All?" I questioned. "Oh you mean Inderal I started for your hypertension." "Yeah." (true story)

...

My wife and I never go to bed angry. I think it's most important to solve the problems before you go to sleep. Last year, I didn't get to bed until December.

...

Donna said to me, "You know that nice couple next door, every morning when he goes to work he gives her a hug and kiss. When he comes home at night he brings her a dozen roses. Why can't you do that?" "Jez,I hardly know her, honey."

...

A lot of people ask why the success of our marriage. I tell them once a week we go out for some candlelight, dinner and dancing. She goes Friday and I go Saturday. (Henny Youngman)

...

That man is so cheap he wouldn't give a nickel to the March of Dimes.

...

I heard Tom Thumb gave Mother Goose the finger.

...

Uncle Beduch is the oldest war protester. He wanted us to pull our troops out of Valley Forge.

...

After his diagnosis, one of my patients wanted to know why I started humming taps.

...

How do I stand Doc? I said, "I'll be damned if I know, I'll attribute it to drink." So the patient remarked, "I'll come back when you're sober, Doc."

...

Longevity runs in Beduch's family. His mother died at 101, thank God they saved the baby.

...

I always liked medicine even at an early age. When I played doctor with the little girls, they always made me play the anesthesiologist.

...

Beduch will donate his body to the Albany Medical Center when he dies. But the Medical Center is contesting the will.

...

A call came to me while driving on the Northway. It was my wife with a message to be careful. She heard there a car driving the wrong way on the Northway. I said, "Hell no, there's a whole bunch." "By the way, how did the baby carriage get on my hood?"

...

Gertrude, the elephant at the zoo, died and her keeper was crying hysterically. I said, "I didn't know you were that close to Gert." "I'm not, but I have to bury her!"

...

They found a skeleton in the closet at Ellis Hospital. I think it was the winner of their 1955 Hide and Go Seek contest.

...

For Christmas this year, I bought my wife a carving set: Three chisels and a mallet!

...

Did I tell you that I met my wife at a shoplifters convention?

...

While I was practicing the piano last night there was a knock at the door and I answered it. "Who are you?" "I'm the piano tuner." "I didn't call a piano tuner.." "No, your neighbors did!"

...

I'm telling you, the wait time at the Ellis Hospital emergency room is a long one. I was there last week taking care of a fractured forearm and the patient in front of me was from Saratoga... the Battle of Saratoga. It was a musket wound.

...

I saw my very old friend, Jack at the bar last night doing shots. Shots of formaldehyde.

...

My old friend is such a bad driver the police gave him a season ticket.

...

Jack the Ripper's mother said to him, "How come I never see you with the same woman?"

...

Do your children suffer from *dependicitis*?

...

I've had a lot of patients at death's door and pulled them through.

...

Last week in the office, I said, "Lady I don't like the way your husband looks." "Well neither do I, but he is awfully good to the kids."

...

I saw a very obese person in the office infected with a flesh-eating bacteria. I gave him three years to live.

...

Do you know any engineers that if you ask the time, they tell you how to build a watch? I do.

...

My multiple-marriage buddy tells me when he can't sleep, he counts his wives.

...

Trump is an alpha male on beta-blockers.

...

It's tough to be nostalgic when you can't remember anything.

...

The food at the restaurant we went to last night was so bad, I gave the doggie bag to my dog and he immediately started licking his butt. I guess he wanted to get the taste out of his mouth.

...

Ken Burns of PBS has a new documentary called *The Great Cabbage Fart Of 1861*. It is a penetrating look at history.

...

Beduch is not a handsome man. His kids draw straws to see who has to kiss him good night.

...

I think you should go to the veterinarian and get your distemper shot.

...

One of the patients asked me how his health was. I replied, "I would suggest you don't buy anything on time."

...

I called my doctor the other day to tell him I had diarrhea and he put me on hold.

...

It was so cold in Albany last night I had to undress with an ice pick.

...

On my call to my urologist's office the receptionist said, "Can you hold please?" "That 's why I'm calling!" I screamed.

...

Remember ladies, if it has tires and testicles you're gonna have a problem with it.

...

One of my patients told me when he awoke from surgery, "Your face was the first thing I saw, Doc" and I said, "I bet you thought you died and went to hell."

...

To help lower car insurance costs, my wife took a offensive driving course.

...

He is the kind of guy that would throw a beer party and throw away the key to the restroom.

...

The twins celebrated their birthday and anniversary of their first apartment together with their Mom.

...

My wife says I'm not a good lover but at least I'm fast.

...

That man is so mean he would give Rolaids indigestion.

...

My friend Sam went home and found his best friend in bed with his wife. He says "Sid, I have to …but you?"

...

Hey buddy, I found out that we are neighbors, I looked at the registered sex offender list and saw your name there.

...

Beduch's wife took off her makeup and the poor dog threw up. He said she was sent from heaven to make his life a living hell.

...

She asked him, "How come you came home half drunk last night?" "Because I ran out of money," he said.

...

MOSTLY ONE LINERS CAUSE I CAN'T REMEMBER TWO...

I said to Donna, "Will you love me when I am old, fat and ugly?" She said "I do."

...

The eyewitnesses were on the scene in minutes.

...

I'm appalled you would say that, Vinnie. Blondes have feelings too.

...

That man is so skinny, if he turned sideways he would be marked absent.

...

I think Donald Trump suffers from "I" disease.

...

Will Rogers said he never met a man he didn't like. I guess he never met Donald.

...

Mother buried three husbands. Unfortunately, two were only sleeping.

...

Listening to that man is like staring at a cow for 45 minutes.

...

After 12 years of psychotherapy my psychiatrist said something that brought a tear to my eye, "No hablo Ingles."

...

Our piano player broke his wrist. Unfortunately, I set it crooked and now he plays a little flat with the left hand.

. . .

If you can tell a man by the friends he keeps. I would say I am in real trouble.

. . .

I asked the patient if he had any of cardiac disease. He told me a cardiac "castration" and they put in three "stenches." His workup included a pulmonary "blow job."(pulmonary function test) (true story.)

. . .

Such a pretty girl, if only I was young and strong.

. . .

At one of the band performances, there was a particularly small crowd and when we completed the number I thanked the audience for the "clap." The crowd was smaller than the orchestra and it was a three-piece band.

. . .

Homosexuality in Russia is a crime. The punishment is seven years in prison locked up with other men. So far there's a three-year waiting list.

. . .

A man walked into the bar "with an AK-47 and said, "Where's the man that's been fooling with my wife?" The bartender replied, "Buddy you better have a lot of bullets."

. . .

Confucius says:
> *Even a blind squirrel finds an acorn once in a while.*
> *Sleep with dogs and wake up with fleas.*
> *You can't learn to swim without getting in the water.*
> *You must row with the oars that you have been given.*
> *Little boats should stay close to the shore.*

. . .

In Murphy's Bar the men's room that has an express line. Over the first urinal there is a sign that says five beers or less. Now that's a good idea.

. . .

You want me to kiss you under the mistletoe? Hell, I wouldn't kiss you under anesthesia.

. . .

Beduch has written in his will that his wife must remarry in the event of his death. So there'll be at least one other person that will regret his death.

. . .

The play I went to see the other night was so bad, I asked the lady in front of me to put her hat back on.

. . .

After my last colonoscopy I asked the doctor to write my wife a note and tell her that my head wasn't up there. I also asked if there where any signs of the trapped miners?

. . .

Sometimes it's harder to deal with success than failure.

. . .

Keep your head up in failure and down in success.

. . .

For our anniversary I told my wife, "Let's go out and have some fun, if you get home before I do, leave the light on."(Rodney Dangerfield)

. . .

The state of Arizona just passed a the law that says it's okay to use a silencer on your 357 Magnum pistol, I guess, during a home invasion they don't want you disturbing the neighbors.

. . .

MOSTLY ONE LINERS CAUSE I CAN'T REMEMBER TWO...

I used to have fun while at the office with the young kids. Often they were very nervous and when I would ask their name they would often stumble. I would then say, "Take your time the questions get tougher. You can check your underwear it might be printed there." I would also step on the scale while the nurse would check their weight and see how upset the teenagers got when they were so overweight.

...

Do you think George Strait is gay?

...

After you're kissed at a party say, "Be careful I have a lip fungus that hasn't been identified yet." Then watch the reaction.

...

Go ahead and play the blues if it'll make you happy.

...

People ask Beduch how long has he been married? He says, "Over 50 years, but don't applaud, you haven't seen her yet."

...

A hooker told Beduch once "Not now, I have a headache."(Rodney Dangerfield)

...

Was it George Bush called the Pope to wish him a happy Passover?

...

My granddaughter's boyfriend asked her, "Is there were someone else? She replied "God there must be. You think I'd be hanging around with a loser like you, if there were."

. . .

My wife can be a bad cook. When she serves the food, we clear the table and bury the dead. She was not happy one night when I asked, "Who was coming *to* dinner, the paramedics?"

. . .

When a new funeral director is asked how businesses and they say good. Is that good or bad? I have been wondering that since I saw her new advertisement.

. . .

When I was a baby, I was kidnapped and a ransom was demanded. But my family would not pay. They didn't want to break a ten.

. . .

This place makes Mayberry look like a think tank.

. . .

When Columbus arrived in America he wanted to buy the land from the Indians, but couldn't get any money. The banks were closed for Columbus Day.

. . .

Donna said to me recently, "When we got married I cried, why didn't you?" I said to her, "I've cried every day since."

. . .

In my Italian Catholic family when I went to confession for the first time, I asked my dad what to say? And dad replied, "Don't tell him nothin'... you didn't see nothin'.... you didn't hear nothin'... tell him you weren't there!"

...

I asked my friend when he came to visit from Mississippi, "How come it took so long to get here?" He told me "It normally is a two day trip, but it took an entire day to spell Schenectady right for his GPS."

...

I had one family in my practice that had so many children there was standing room only in the playpen. I think it was 10.

...

My granddaughter was dating the captain of the chess team in high school. Her parents liked that a lot. They figured anybody it takes three hours to make a move is got to be okay.

...

I'd like you to meet my good friend and partner Dr. Patel and his lovely wife Patella.

...

A friend of mine has gotten so fat, he can't even get into his own pants.

...

Doris Day was so pure that even Moses couldn't part her legs. Groucho Marx said that he knew her before she was a virgin.

...

I enjoyed listening to Mozart's clarinet Concerto in A. It was quite beautiful. The conductor told me what a wonderful composer Mozart was. I said, "That's great, but what has he written recently?"

...

Beduch's wife said, "You like the dog better than me. You greet her first when you come home." Beduch replied, "If you'd shake your ass at me like she does, I'd scratch your belly too."

...

I was talking to a friend of mine from Scotland about how he liked the neighbors. He said he didn't like them because they were noisy, pounded on the wall and screamed all night." "How do you handle it?" "I lie on my bed and play my bagpipe."

...

I'm talking dumb, he couldn't direct traffic on a one-way street. I told him I couldn't believe out of 10,000 sperm he was the fastest.

...

If dumb ever goes $200 a barrel I want drilling rights to your head.

...

Politicians are similar to diapers. Both need changing regularly and for the same reason.

...

You know you're depressed when you're reading obituaries to cheer up. (Donna)

...

I read a couple of interesting books: one was on the *History of Glue*, I couldn't put it down. The other one was called *The Boy Who Died from Eating All of his Vegetables*.

...

When listening to a song written by a rival composer, Johnny Mercer said that he could eat alphabet soup and shit better lyrics.

...

The inventor the bagpipes was inspired when he saw a man carrying an indignant asthmatic pig under his arm. Unfortunately, the man-made device never equaled the purity of sound obtained by the pig.

...

Science has shown for three days after death the hair and nails continue to grow but the calls from the medical exchange start to drop off.

...

A doctor friend of mine died and I went to the funeral. As they were lowering the casket into the grave, I heard a buzzing. I said to the widow, "What was that?" She said, "That's his cell phone, he is on call this weekend."

...

Congratulations on your new baby. Do you know who the father is?

...

He's a great guy. He tells me that all the time.

...

Being bisexual means you get twice the number of dates.

...

Beduch got arrested for having indecent material. The arresting officer said, "Hey, you got any decent stuff?"

...

When I die, I've instructed Donna to donate my organs: three trumpets, one banjo and 15 accordions to science. Unfortunately no one wants the accordions.

...

After babysitting my daughter Heather's twins, my wife came home and said "I must be doing something right, they both said they hate me."

...

Advice on which doctors to avoid; Someone whose office plants all have died, has a street in the cemetery named after him, and "Born to Lose" tattooed on his knuckles.

...

The doctor walks in to examine you and his lab coat buttons are misaligned, he flunks the test. You don't want him doing your brain surgery.

...

I think you should have a pimp for brother so you have someone to look up to.

...

Beduch's personality is like Al Capone, but he lacks his compassion.

...

Home Depot has a tool for every purpose. They even have one for treatment of depression. It's called a *coping saw*.

. . .

Beduch spent $150 at Amazon for a penis enlarger. They sent him a magnifying glass.

. . .

I wish I could pee like my wife spends money.

. . .

That's kind of like asking a chicken to vote for Col. Sanders.

. . .

Never trust a nun with a boner.

. . .

It was so cold last week, I saw three dogs stuck to a fire hydrant.

. . .

Beduch looks more confused than a baby in a topless bar.

. . .

I've been in the doghouse so many times that when I get out and meet other people, I don't know whether to shake their hand or sniff their crotch.

. . .

My granddaughter graduated with honors from Harvard School of Business and I am pleased to tell you she already has landed her first job. She will be working in management for the Colonie Mall. It'll be at the food court with Hot Dog On-A-Stick.

. . .

When I was in college I brought my girlfriend home for the weekend and my mother asked whether she would be sleeping in the spare bedroom or the kennel. Golly, she even put papers in the floor.

. . .

I guess she wasn't very pretty. When she was born, the incubator had tinted windows.

. . .

My niece had a habit of dating very young men. She awoke one morning and looked at who was next to her and said, " Was this my date or did I give birth last night?"(Joan Rivers)

...

Ah, my friend Jack Spring, forgotten but not gone.

...

I think you inherited your big boobs from your father, but don't feel too bad, your friend's dad said he beat his daughter by 2 cup sizes.

...

My wife was complaining that I never tell her I love her. "I told you over 50 years ago that I love you if anything changes, I'll be sure to let you know" I said.

...

They discharged me from the psych hospital for depressing the other patients.

...

Sometimes after big bowel movement, Beduch feels like he has dropped two pants sizes. It was the biggest evacuation since Dunkirk.

...

Is there a seniors' discount at Hooters? My good friend goes there for the food.

...

I am so glad that Jack Spring is here tonight to speak. We couldn't get anybody else.

...

Jesus was laid in a manger because there was no room in the Inn. Gosh, wouldn't you think Mary and Joseph would know you couldn't get a room on a holiday.

...

Sometimes my daughter is a bad cook, so we bought her an oven that flushes.

...

Our band's fan club broke up last week.... The man died.

...

Beduch's wife went to the plastic surgeon. He took one look and wanted to add a tail. Her face has been pulled up more times than Bill Clinton's zipper. A sign outside the surgeon's office said: *A Scar is Born*. Beduch's wife is on 14th year of the 10-day beauty plan.

...

When that singer hit the high C on the Star-Spangled Banner it spayed my dog.

...

The patient came to see me with a deformed arm and I took an x-ray. It was fractured, but I also told her it was healed. I asked, "Why didn't she see me sooner." She said, "It took me six weeks to get an appointment."

...

When you read the obituaries, isn't amazing to see that the people die in alphabetical order.

...

Doctor, doctor there is a strawberry growing out of the top of my head. Don't worry I'll give you some cream to put on it.

...

Another patient came to see me and I diagnosed a bad case of HAGS disease. He asked, "What's that?" "That's herpes, aids, gonorrhea and syphilis and is treated by complete isolation and a diet of pancakes and bacon." "Pancakes and bacon, why is that?" "It's the only food we can slide under the door!"

...

My wife says I never listen, at least that's what I thought she said.

...

I knew our marriage was off to a bad start when at the wedding service the priest said, "You may kiss the bride." And Donna said, "Not now I've got a headache."

...

The neighborhood I was born in was so dangerous that even the serial killers went around in pairs.

...

Beduch's good health he attributes to a carefully controlled diet of cigarettes and alcohol.

...

"Hey Nick, you've already been married twice, why again?" "I miss the cheating."

...

Police are searching for persons with a motive for killing Tony. So far they have found 33,000 suspects.

...

I got home from the gym recently I said to my wife, "I feel like a new man." She commented quickly "So do I."

...

As Beduch was checking out at Walmart, and the cashier said to him, " Have a good one." He said "I'd love a good one, it's been so long and I'm so lonely." The cashier replied, "You disgusting old man."

...

I had one patient that had a persistent cough, so I gave her a laxative to take. Puzzled, she asked, "How is this going to help?" "It won't help the cough, but you will be afraid to cough."

...

When coming home from work a few years ago, there was a traffic jam and I inquired to the police officer what the problem was. He replied there's a lawyer blocking the road and says he's bankrupt. He needs money and will set himself on fire unless he gets money. So we are taking up a collection for him. So far we have gotten ten matchbooks and eight lighters.

...

One morning I stepped on the scale and sucked in my stomach. Donna said, "That's not going to help." I said ,"Yes it is, I can read the numbers better." Out came the reading, it said, "One at a time please."

...

If you don't laugh at trouble, you'll have nothing to laugh at when you get old.

...

Old Uncle Beduch has started reading the Bible recently. I guess he's studying for his finals.

...

Actually one patient said to me while asking for a prescription for an antibiotic. " Didn't you used to be a real doctor before you were an orthopedist?"(true story)

...

Our band plays a lot of retirement communities and the following is a list of the most frequently requested numbers:
1. Don't get around much anymore
2. Try to remember
3. Yesterday when I was young
4. What are you doing the rest of your life
5. It's easy to forget but so hard to remember
6. As time goes by

...

A lot of companies must like my voice on the telephone. They are always telling me this call will be recorded and may be used to train other people.

...

I've developed a little shake recently. It's a good thing I don't do circumcisions anymore or direct an orchestra.

...

At my age, even if you still got it no one wants it.

...

Beduch had developed a limp, and went to buy ice cream. He ordered double chocolate cone. The clerk said, "You want crushed nuts?" Beduch responded "Hell no, the arthritis is enough."

...

I was inquiring to one of my Jewish friends if his circumcision was painful. He said ,"I was only eight days old when it was done, so I don't remember. But I can tell you one thing, I didn't walk for a year and a half."

...

During my residency I spent three months as a neurosurgical resident. My first case was ten hours long. It turned out to be a no-brainer. (That's called gallows humor. It helps deal with very painful situations, especially in medicine.)

...

While out with several of our friends, one of the ladies previously thrice married noticed a man at the bar. She went up to him and said, "Pardon me you look familiar, was I married to you once?"

...

Did you ever notice on the animal adoption pages how many pit bull mixes there are listed. They're a pretty aggressive breed. It seems to me a lot of sexual assault has been going on. I saw one mix that was particularly noteworthy. It was a pit bull - domestic short hair mix. I'm telling you it was ugly!

...

After a particularly difficult operation following a motorcycle accident I talked to the very apprehensive mother and told her about the procedure. She asked me, "Is he going to live doctor.?" I said, "Yes he is Mrs. Funderburke." She said, "Good 'cause I'm going to kill him. I told him not to ride that motorcycle!" (true story)

...

A dog is a man's best friend. This alone is quite depressing.

...

My 16-year-old grandson is a very confident young man. He started a little black book listing all his girlfriends' names and email addresses and put volume one on the cover.

...

My wife was on the phone recently. I knew it was going to be a long conversation. She changed ears.

...

My wife received a thank you note from our five-year-old granddaughter Lilah, for the Christmas present. She said in the note, "Thank you for the Christmas present Nonnie, it is something I've always wanted, but not very much."

...

My friend received his Doctorate in Inhumane Letters from Union College for his tuba playing.

...

Is a Rookie Nookie a novice prostitute?

...

The elephants at Ringling Circus refused to perform because they were tired of working for peanuts.

...

My cousin Tony started a broccoli farm, because he heard the price of gas was going up.

...

I was telling a story to my friend on the telephone and apparently got one detail wrong. My wife overheard it and corrected me. In frustration, I said, "We've been married 50 years. You never miss an opportunity to correct me." She said "51!"

...

Doctors say that fatal diseases are the worst.

...

We went to a wedding recently and when the minister said you may kiss the bride and they were very passionate about it. I yelled from the church pew, "Kiss her.... don't kill her!"

...

Is your phone number still the same, 911?

...

Recently, I learned just because you finish the music first, it doesn't mean you are the best musician.

...

The conductor also told me if you have any left-over notes when everyone is done, don't play them.

...

When my granddaughter applied for her job the application asked if she had any special skills that were not listed. She wrote on the application: I can pick up quarters with my toes.

...

An over-privileged arrogant child was in the office waiting to be seen. She said, "Do you know who my father is." I replied indignantly, "No do you?"

...

"Sorry your husband died Mrs. Adams, were there any last requests?" the priest asked. She said "Yeah, 'Put the gun down, Mabel!' "

...

One of my cars is so old when I get it registered at the DMV they give me upper and lower plates.

...

As the old cliché says, "Nothing's cheap nowadays,".... well except maybe me.

...

It's a good thing I see my dentist annually. The tube of toothpaste he gave me is almost gone.

...

A euphemism was used after my recent automobile accident with the other driver. We were involved in some *nonverbal communication.* In other words he gave me the finger.

...

My accountant told me to list all my income for tax purposes for the year. I asked him if I had to include the $28 I got for bottle deposits returns.

...

"Call your brother Paul" Donna said. "That's what I call him. It's his name!"

...

Abraham Lincoln said, "To ease another man's heart ache is to forget one's own."

...

That man has a personality of the potato.

...

Did I tell you Rose Bush got the job as our new gardener?

...

Do you suppose spiders have websites?

...

Last fall, I was buying corn at our roadside stand and I said to the sales clerk, "I have three ears." She looked at me strangely and said," You know I thought you looked a little funny."

...

An elderly gentleman was in the office several years ago and I examined him for complaint he had with his back. And I assured him that it was normal at his age. "At 95, normal for my age is dead, doctor," he said.

...

Before I lost some weight, I was quite heavy. When I got on the Southwest Airlines plane the stewardess said, "We have reserved seat 20-21 and 22 for you."

...

My Jewish friend said he went camping with his wife. "I thought Jews didn't go camping" I said, "We do, only we have it catered."

...

The poor priests nowadays are so old and working really hard. I feel sorry for them. When I meet some of them, I don't know whether to shake their hand or call 911.

...

When my brother's daughter got married several years ago. Her fiancé asked my brother for his daughter's hand in marriage. Paul said, "Certainly you may have her hand, but what's wrong with the rest of her?"

...

As many of you know I enjoy antique cars. I had a beautiful 1949 Chrysler wooden station wagon. My niece was admiring our newly remodeled kitchen. I told her that, "I sold my 49 Chrysler and used the money for the remodeling." "I had a woody." I told her. My lovely wife said, "If you had a woody, that would be the first time in 20 years!"

...

You're not looking good when you drive your 1911 Model T Ford to an antique car show and some smarty-pants youngster asks if you are the original owner?

...

There was man at a cocktail party that remembered I had saved his wife's life 20 years ago. He's never forgiven me.

...

My grandson Jackson was sitting on my lap and patting my bald head. Then he noticed my beard and asked "Bepa, why is your hair upside down?"(true story)

...

Beduch is returning his waterbed to the mattress company. He says his wife's side is frozen.

...

I was taught to respect my elders but it's getting tougher and tougher to find one.

. . .

My wife used to play the guitar but now she picks on me.

. . .

When Beduch was a kid he was hitchhiking to school and got beat up by one of the drivers. He was using the wrong finger.

. . .

Jack the Zipper hangs around funeral parlors to pick up the new widows.

. . .

Daughter Jill asked me if I've heard from our neighbor Robert. I told her, "Not much since he died three weeks ago." (true story)

. . .

Old Beduch got arrested recently for flashing. It got settled in small claims court.

. . .

I took my wife to Alaska for our 25th anniversary. I will bring her back for our 50th.

. . .

After one particular Mexican meal (refried beans) I had a lot of gas. One man said, "How dare you fart before my wife." I said, "I didn't know it was her turn."(Groucho)

. . .

One of my friends said to me, "Jack, who was that woman I saw you with the last night?" "That was no woman, it was my brother-in-law and we're sick about it."

...

I was invited to my neighbor's six-year-old daughter's piano recital. I told her I'd love to go but I have to rearrange my sock drawer.

...

They say everybody needs a dream and I'm pleased to tell you my 96-year-old grandmother just entered medical school... as a cadaver.

...

The oldest man in the concert band plays the biggest instrument, the Sousaphone. As you might expect, he sometimes has difficulty handling it. Being the empathetic man I am, I offered to carry his mouthpiece. What a guy!

...

I looked at my wife's finger and I said, "You 've got your ring on the wrong finger." She looked at me and said, "I've got the wrong husband."

...

I remember my brother Paul asking his orthopedic brother about the large bump on his big toe. "Why that's Paul's Bunion," I told him.

...

Beduch's comment was, "Thank God I'm an atheist."

...

When I signed up for the gym, I looked so bad they asked me to go in the back entrance.

...

Grandpa Spring used to drink a wee bit. He was bombed before Pearl Harbor.

...

When Grandpa died, he wanted to be buried at sea. He had retired from the Navy and six men drown digging his grave.

...

Sign: HONEST CARR.... USED JOHN SALESMAN.
Sign at new hair salon: CURL UP AND DYE!

...

I was saying to my wife how loud some of the other trumpet players are playing. She said, "Jack, they're just trying to cover up your mistakes." (Donna)

...

I was also complaining that I wasn't happy with my trumpet playing. Donna said, "You don't sound any worse than you ever did." (Donna)

...

The Chinese fortune cookie I got after the meal said, "Help, I'm a prisoner in a Chinese cookie factory."

...

There is no to soon, only too late. So when you think of it, call your friends. Don't wait.

...

My dear wife says, "I'm not fat, but only retaining water." "Retaining water? Hell, it seems like I'm retaining Lake Michigan."

...

You say you think I'm getting fat? The reason is every time your wife and I get together, she gives me a biscuit. By the way you have a lovely home, but you were out of scotch.

...

Please don't blame your wife, it's my fault. I answered her ad in the Schenectady Gazette.

...

I finally met the girl of my dreams, I could not ask for more. She was deaf and blind and oversexed And owned a liquor store! (Thank you Dean Martin)

...

I tried almond milk yesterday and it wasn't too bad. But how in the hell do you milk an almond!

...

The psychiatrist told Beduch that he didn't have an inferiority complex. He told him he was inferior.

...

My comment to wealthy conceited young woman: You are such a beautiful young woman, my compliments to your surgeon. Even the bags under your eyes look like they were made by Gucci.

...

Two cowboys are riding together in Indian country and they hear drums in the distance. One says to the other, "I don't like the sounds of those drums." From across the canyon a voice yells "Sorry, he's not our regular drummer."

...

Old man Methuselah got married to a very young woman. I asked, "What'd ya give her for a wedding present, blocks and crayons?"

...

My daughter brought her fiancé home for me to meet. I looked and said, "So this is the man you're going to marry...... he looks like he'll make a good first husband."

...

Note to husband: "Come home darling, forgive and forget. I have destroyed the chili recipe. Love Mabel."

...

I've been asked many times why I play the trumpet. I play for my amazement and revenge.

...

Rock musicians usually play with three chords for thousands of people and jazz musicians play thousands of chords for three people.

...

In the orchestra I used to play first chair, but when I couldn't put my lips around the seat anymore, they moved me down to the smaller second chair.

...

Be careful, my BS detector is going off. I should call you the Ernest Hemmingway of bull shit.

...

I have been drinking a special soft drink since I have entered my senior years. I use it for a laxative. It is called Doctor Pooper.

...

Recently on my flight to Tucson I sat next to a behemoth. She needed three seatbelt extenders, and that was just for her thighs.

...

It was a horrible flight. I sat next to a crying baby and the damn thing was smoking!

...

Beduch's wife has flabby thighs, but fortunately her belly covers them up.

...

They named a Jewish holiday after Beduch's sex life -- Passover!

...

Boy that's a big tattoo! Was it was financed with a 30-year adjustable rate mortgage?

...

The paparazzi spotted Kate and William on the Royal yacht sunbathing. She was topless. They are keeping an eye on the royal pair.

...

Now that I'm retired a lot of people ask whether I miss medicine. I usually tell them, " No, medicine has changed too much. They won't let me bleed and purge anymore."

...

My patient told me his eyes water every time he has sex. I told him it's probably the MACE.

...

Beduch tells me he hides his money from his wife underneath the vacuum cleaner.

...

The wife of Beduch is currently expecting a baby. She has collected a list of names. I'm sure she will find the father there somewhere.

...

Two men were sentenced to die in the electric chair and each was given one last request. One man was a musician and he requested that he might be allowed to play his bagpipes one last time. The other man quickly said, "Please let me go first!"

...

Last week I went to an Irish wake and at the viewing, I said to the widow, "Your husband looks wonderful." "He should, he hasn't had a drink in 3 days."

...

To save a little money when the children were small, I used to tell the kids when the ice cream truck played music it was out of ice cream.

...

Facing the gallows in Syria, a compassionate guard asked the condemned prisoner if he would like a cigarette. "No thanks, I'm trying to cut down."

...

I know a smoker that has read so much about the harmful effects of smoking, he gave up reading.

...

When I was kissed by a vegetarian I got terribly sick. It must've been the wheat germ.

...

Research shows that the first five minutes of life are quite risky. As a physician, I can tell you the last five ain't so hot either.

...

Doctor Spring, my mom must really like you. She even put her teeth in for you. (true story)

...

Queen Elizabeth says she doesn't care where people make love, just as long as they don't do it in the street and scare the horses.

...

When men get older, it becomes more difficult and takes longer to void. The advertising industry has made a note and now is advertising over men's urinals in the restroom. They figure that you might as well read something while peeing. A few weeks ago, I had time to read Tolstoy's *War and Peace*.

...

Daughter Lisa's dog Spot is blind. She calls him Blind Spot.

...

Donna and I went on a beautiful vacation to Bermuda. When we got off the airplane we heard drums, when we got to the hotel we heard drums, at the front desk we heard drums and even at the restaurant more drums. I finally said to the maître' d, "My God, when do these drums stop?" The maître d' anxiously said "very bad when drum stop......... bass solo begins!"

...

I was a little heavy as a kid. I went bungee jumping off a bridge and pulled it over.

...

Beduch and his wife recently have been facing financial hardship in their retirement. They decided that she would help the family income by working as a prostitute. She was exhausted on the first night when she returned home. She told her husband she had earned only $25.10. Beduch asked, "Who gave you $.10?" She said "EVERYBODY!"

...

At orchestra rehearsal last week, the conductor Vince yelled, "Hey Doc, you are doing better, you got all the right notes this time, just in the wrong places."

...

A midget I know came up to a beautiful woman at the bar and said that he would like to make love to her. She said, "If you do and I find out about it, I'm calling the police."

...

When old Beduch was dating his wife, he asked her if he was the first man she ever made love to. She thought for a minute and said, "Come to think of it, you do look familiar. Why does everybody ask me that?"

...

Old uncle Beduch tried phone sex but the poor guy ended up with an ear infection. And when he got the phone bill it was astronomical. He got a girl that stuttered.

...

Beduch calls his wife his "significant other" and she refers to him as her "insignificant other."

...

In Jerusalem there was an old Jew who had been going to the Wailing Wall twice a day for 50 years and praying for peace between the Arabs and Jews. He wanted their children to grow up with friendship and safety. A CNN reporter asked, "Isaac, how does it feel after praying so long for peace?" "Like I'm talking to a Goddamn wall!"

...

Since my retirement I often go out to lunch with some of my old friends. Some are still working, some are not. When the check came, I offered to pay. My friend said, "I won't hear of it. You haven't earned a paycheck in 10 years."

...

Last winter with a severe head cold, I was bellyaching about my stuffed head. I said to my wife, a former nurse, " I need something to clear my head. "She said, "Try a 357 magnum Smith & Wesson."

...

In my first year of surgical residency at Georgetown things were quite overwhelming. I was working on the open heart unit and the patient that we had just finished replacing an aortic valve on had died and two others in the cardiac ICU were critical. I was just completing a 72-hour shift and was completely exhausted. While walking into the ICU I saw a sign hanging on the wall. It reassuringly said, "Smile, Jesus loves you." But what really made me laugh hysterically was handwritten note below, "But the rest of us think you're an idiot!"(true story)

...

Early in my surgical training, I was trying to balance long hours with our new marriage. As you might expect, Donna was feeling a little neglected. So she found a perfume at Lord and Taylor, that smelled like the operating room (Simple Green and Chlorox)!

...

It is easier to ask for forgiveness than ask for permission.

...

The orchestra was going to perform Franz Schubert's Symphony No. 8 in B minor but we couldn't because he hadn't "finished" it yet! Jez, he's been working on it over a hundred years.

...

When I was in high school I was a big hairy kid. One of the young girls was quite pretty, so I decided to ask her for a date. She said, "Sorry buddy I don't date outside my species."

...

While walking on the street recently, a man stopped me and said, "What's the fastest way to the Walmart store?" I asked, "Are you walking or driving?" He said "Driving." I said, "That's the fastest way."(Steven Wright)

...

You have between your legs the most sensitive instrument known to man and all you can do is scratch it.   (Conductor Sir Thomas Beecham to the female cellist)

...

It's easier to suffer in silence if you're sure someone is watching.

...

I went to my 50th class reunion from high school and saw a woman I thought I recognized. I went up to her and said, "You look like Helen Brown." She looked at me and said, "Well your orange suit doesn't look so great either, buddy."

...

At the same reunion a gal from the class came up to me and remarked, "Look at you Jack Richards, you've gained weight, got a beard and now you're bald." "I'm sorry lady, I'm not Jack Richards." "I don't believe it, you also changed you name!"

...

Our bass player doesn't know his brass from his oboe.

...

You can never go home again. No matter how hard you try. (Unfortunately)

...

Last month the frame on my glasses fell apart and I took it to an optician to fix it. I told the lady there that it needed a screw. She looked at me and said, "Who doesn't?"

...

You are not punished for your sins. But you are punished *by* your sins.

...

Don't tell my mother I'm a doctor. She thinks I play the piano in a whorehouse.

...

The priest asked, "Have you ever slept with a woman?" "Father, I've dozed off a couple of times."

...

Most people die of natural causes, so I am looking for a cure for natural causes.

...

Heart surgeons have successfully transplanted a turtle heart into a human at the Cleveland Clinic. The patient was discharged from the hospital two weeks ago. So far he has made it to their parking lot.

...

My wife became extremely ill so I decided to call 911. The operator answers and asks " Where do you live doctor?" "24 Eucalyptus Drive" I replied. "Can you spell that please?" she asked. "Spelling isn't my strong suit, why don't I drag her over to Oak Street."

...

A promiscuous young woman in the office told me that she needed a kidney transplant and was worried it might not take. I told her no need to worry, her body hasn't rejected an organ in twenty-five years.

...

One lady told me her hard working husband was a work alcoholic. (true story)

...

When I was in high school I played sousaphone in the football team marching band. You can bet the cheerleaders were all over me.

...

One of the girls that I had for a secretary was a problem. I told her, "Chris you have to answer the phone and don't let it ring." She said, "Why, most of the time it's for you." She was so insecure, when she did answer, she would say, "Hello, can you help me?"

...

Chris is so strongly involved in recycling that she wouldn't consider marriage unless the man has been married before.

...

Surprising as it may seem, Beduch's wife never appreciated his unique ability to fart the theme song from *Gunsmoke*. I was impressed, but the second measure was a little flat.

...

When my friend was recently hospitalized he got better when he took a "turn for the nurse."

...

When I was a kid, discipline by my parents was to treat my backside to a spanking with a wooden spoon. I'm not complaining and it was quite effective. Hell, I used to call it my father's "Weapon of Ass Destruction."

...

I'm on Jennie Craig. If my wife finds out she'll kill me.

...

As I was practicing the trumpet, Donna yelled, "What are you paying for lessons?" "Forty dollars an hour," I said. "I'll give you sixty to stop!" she loudly responded. (Donna)

...

I'm telling you Kamikaze Airline's planes are really old. The last one I flew had an outside toilet.

...

I told a elderly lady patient I was retiring and laughed when she replied, "Was it something I said?" (true story)

...

I went to a funeral mass for an old friend. After the service when I was talking to the priest and he asked how old I was. After I told him, he looked at me and said "Jack, you might just as well stay here."

...

My wife and I had a slight disagreement last week. I argued, "Where are you going to find another man like me?" She said, "In a mental hospital!"

...

Honey, I love the sweater. It's a good thing you never throw anything out. (It wasn't a good night.)

...

I so hairy as a kid, I had to take a bath with a vacuum cleaner. Mom always said, "John, comb your face." Now I'm bald, go figure.

...

Last week at the gym I was in the weight room and listening to some of those gorillas grunt. I didn't know if they were lifting weights, having sex or trying for a bowel movement. I even offered one a banana. (He didn't like that.) They can't even walk by a mirror without adoring themselves. They will probably die in their own arms.

...

Both the women and men at Gold's Gym have so many tattoos it looks like they were attacked by a Home Depot paint salesman.

...

Since my retirement I spend a lot of time going out to lunch with my buddies. Gee Whiz, I've gained twenty pounds from so many lunches.

...

One lunch group I belong to is called the RODEO Club, Retired Old Doctors Eating Out.

...

Discussions at these luncheons sounds more like a organ recital. "My kidney hurts, my heart is failing, I can't feel my feet and my back hurts so baaaad I can hardly walk. But you know me, I can't complain!"

...

I've been happily married over 50 years...my wife about 6 months.

...

The gym has an area labeled free weights. I took a few.

...

Beduch drinks a wee bit. He got home late one night with slurred speech. He explained to his wife someone had stepped on his tongue.

...

In the neighborhood where I was born, safe sex meant locking all the doors.

...

Spring ahead and fall back is the way to remember how to change the clock, but to me it's trying to get out of the chair.

...

At one time Beduch thought about running for President but decided not to do it. He was afraid no woman would come forward and admit they had sex with him.

...

At my age, the house is too big and the medicine cabinet is too small. Oh well.

...

Ellis Maternity Hospital has a sign on the birthing room door: "Thank you for removing your rubbers."

...

I asked the barber, "How come a haircut for a bald man costs so much?" "Because it takes so long to find your hairs."

...

I told one patient he had 3 weeks to live. So he held up a bank and the judge gave him 10 years.

...

Waiter, there's soup on my fly.

...

My definition of an alcoholic is a person that drinks more than his doctor.

...

Hanna fell and broke her nose. I x-rayed it and I told her to stay off it.

...

Donna gave me a lovely birthday gift. It was a beautiful monogramed denture cup. Sweet.

...

Beduch's house is messy. Folks wipe their feet after they leave. (Joan Rivers)

...

The plastic surgeon made that actress's lips so big, I think she could French kiss a moose.

...

I never buy the lifetime battery for my watch. Why waste the money?

...

My granddaughter's boyfriend said to her that if she didn't kiss him, he'd blow his brains out. She told him, "You better be a good shot."

...

Sometimes I wonder about Beduch's parents. They told him to take candy from strangers.

...

Joan Rivers says she was pretty innocent as a adolescent. When she started menstruation, she put a tourniquet around her waist. (Joan Rivers)

...

That gal never had any children but she has 2 dogs by a previous marriage.

...

Recently I had a car accident and the man is suing me for a million dollars. From the size of him, it looks like that's one year's grocery bill.

...

That man was 400 lbs. Once he went to a Chinese buffet in one taxi and but had to leave in two. When he came into the place the manager started to tremble.

...

Where there's smoke, there's dinner. Donna uses the smoke alarm as a timer.

...

My good friend Jim graduated from Union College and the school wanted to endow a chair to honor him. Unfortunately, they couldn't raise enough money, so he got a stool.

...

My wife always nags me at the office party when I go back to the buffet table so much. She says, "Doesn't it bother you that people see you getting food so many times, John?" "Naw honey, I tell 'em it's for you."

...

Do you have to leave our party so early? No, it was purely a matter of choice.

...

There are three stages of life: youth, middle age and the "Gee, your looking good," stage.

...

A new bug is attacking our Ash trees. I think the arborist called it an Emerald Ass Borer.

...

When I had coronary artery bypass surgery my wife made a astute observation. She said, "You know John, you are a nicer person since your heart was exposed to the air." (Donna)

...

A woman celebrated her 103rd birthday as noted in the Schenectady Gazette. I figured no big deal, look how long it took her to get there.

...

Science is looking for ways to cut down on cow flatulence. I'd suggest the best way would be ignore them when they ask you to pull their hoof.

. . .

My friend was telling me about his unmotivated 45-year old son. He can't hold a job. "He's been retired all his life, you might say," he said.

. . .

I told my patient she had broken her leg in two places. My advice was not to go to those places again. (Henny Youngman)

. . .

They always say laughter is the best medicine, but I wish I had given the man with pneumonia an antibiotic instead of telling him a funny story.

. . .

An anxious young lady was being examined by me for a painful neck and I asked her to put her left ear on her shoulder. She replied, "Which shoulder?" (true story)

. . .

We're talking old. This is the guy that told Noah, "Don't worry, it's only a sprinkle."

. . .

An angry patient said he waited so long to be seen he forgot the way out. I suggested dropping seeds to mark the path.

. . .

There was a family I knew well and did a total knee replacement on the husband. He was a very big man, probably over 300 pounds. His wife was concerned about bathing him when he went home. I said, "No problem Agnes, just run him through the car wash." (true story)

...

Beduch got pulled over by the cops and the officer said, "Sir, do you know your wife fell out of the car about two miles back?" "Thank God, I thought my hearing had gone."

...

Prior to surgery, I asked a patient if she had a bowel movement. "No doctor, I'm constipated." From the front of the OR table the anesthesiologist loudly yells, "Wait till she gets your bill Jack, she'll shit." He promptly put her under. (true story)

...

The patient returned for follow-up and was complaining he wasn't better. I said, "Have you been taking the medicine I prescribed for you?" "Yes, up the wazoo." "Well, that's why it hasn't helped, you are supposed to take it by mouth." (true story)

...

My niece is pretty thin. She swallowed an olive and 6 guys left town.

...

PMS was described and written about in the Bible. It said, "Mary grabbed Joseph and rode his ass into Bethlehem."

...

I was examining a man and looked at his navel. It was the biggest I had ever seen. "How come you have such a big belly button?" I asked. "Because I used to carry the flag there for the Salvation Army Marching Band."

. . .

When I started playing in the orchestra, the trumpets were seated in front of the trombones until I complained. I kept getting welts on the back of my neck.

. . .

Often our concert band plays at senior living facilities and I see folks that I have operated upon. One evening, I saw lady that had a total hip replacement and I went over to her and asked if she knew who I was. She said, "No I don't, but if you go to the front desk I'm sure they could tell you."

. . .

By the way, never look at the trombones, it only encourages them. (Sir Thomas Beecham)

. . .

We are a bunch of seniors that play in the Albany Area Seniors Orchestra. When we practice it looks like tryouts for the *Antique Road Show* or maybe *American Pickers*.

. . .

Before I went completely bald, I used my ear hairs for a comb over. It looked strange, like I was wearing headphones. Then I tried a toupee and stopped that when I won first prize in the Westminster Kennel Show.

. . .

Our Catholic hospital, St. Clare's, was on a austerity budget. They had to lay off the hospital chaplain. But fortunately, they got a rabbi for less money.

...

"Doctor, can you suggest a good florist? I'd like to buy some flowers for the head nurse." "Why yes, I'm sure she would be pleased," I said. "Pleased hell, I rang the bell an hour and half ago. I thought she was dead."

...

So dumb! He thinks Helen of Troy is a hooker from upstate New York. (Red Buttons)

...

I'm sorry about your wife, do you remember her last words? "Yes, how can they sell this tuna for 25 cents a can?"

...

My grandson got a great job for the summer working in a gym. He will be working as the fog light operator in the steam room.

...

I was practicing the trumpet one evening and the dog started to howl. Donna yelled, "Can't you play something the dog doesn't know."

...

In the office, I saw an 80-year old lady that was dating a 90-year old man. So I asked, "How is it going?" She said, "I had to slap him three times last night." "Was he getting fresh?" "No, I thought he was dead."

...

You're not drunk if you can lie on the floor without holding on. (Dean Martin)

...

My pessimistic partner and I were having a drink during happy hour at our local watering hole. He wasn't there 5 minutes and they asked him to leave.

...

Businesses are looking for help and are having a hard time filling some positions. My granddaughter said she got hired right after the guy with the face tattoo. Wow!

...

Period costume from the 20s is fun when I play with the Dixieland band. I found a great double breasted suit with a vest at a second hand store and wore it on one gig. The tuba player liked the suit and asked where I got it and how much did it cost. I told him, "At the Salvation Army for five dollars." "Let me know when it goes on sale!" he said.

...

Vince, our conductor, said to me last week, " Jack, I can't expect you to be with us all the time, but try to keep in touch once in a while." (Sir Thomas Beachum, conductor)

...

After a moment like that, I feel like a man in a black tuxedo wearing white socks. I stuck out.

...

You're the apple of my eye but the pain in my ass.

...

Last month, as I opened my usually large MasterCard bill. I actually heard a drum roll.

...

The man that invented Crest toothpaste died and 9 out of 10 dentists went to his funeral.

...

Someone asked me what is the difference between the first and second trumpet player. I'd estimate about a measure and a half.

...

You know what happens when the 3rd trumpet player dies? They move him down to 4th.

...

We played a gig last year and people were so pleased with our performance they asked us to play again next year. I told them, "Sure, but only if you have a place we can store our instruments."

...

They also asked us to play an encore, but I told them it was late in the evening. We have to have the fake books back to Hermies Music Store by 10.

...

Over the 4th of July I got a call to play a gig with another band and was quite excited. I happily told my wife my good luck. Donna said, "Don't feel so great John, Dave called 122 other trumpet players and no one else could make it."

...

A cresendo: a reminder that you are playing to loud.
A glissando: a technique to be used for a difficult run.
And vibrato: used when you can't find the right note.

· · ·

Our piano player was with the Philadelphia Symphony Orchestra for 35 years and when he got home his wife didn't recognize him.

· · ·

The conductor yelled at the first violin," Who's sitting in that empty chair?" (Eugene Ormandy)

· · ·

We have a lot of seniors playing in the orchestra and one called to tell the conductor he wouldn't be at practice that day. He had misplaced his teeth. Never heard that one before. Dog ate my teeth, maybe.

· · ·

My first date wasn't very successful. I asked for a goodnight kiss and she bent over. (Rodney Dangerfield)

· · ·

My partner told me he had a great song reflecting my surgical outcomes. Rogers and Hammerstein's "You'll Never Walk Again."

· · ·

Jewish Nativity scene: Five trial lawyers viewing a car accident at Christmas.

· · ·

While I was reading the paper one evening, Donna said, "It's a beautiful night for a walk. The moon is bright, a nice breeze and not to hot." I said, "You know it is, make sure you take the dog."

SOME MORE TRUE STORIES FROM 45 YEARS OF SURGICAL PRACTICE...

Our family had just settled down for a lovely Christmas eve dinner, when the phone rang. It was the St. Clares emergency room and there was a fractured hip. I had to go attend to it. That's when Donna uttered her famous words: "Priests should be married and Doctors shouldn't!"

...

There was a young lad had a fracture of the forearm at the emergency room and I told him we had "to put him asleep" to set his bone correctly. Immediately the child started crying hysterically. "What's wrong?" I said to the mother. "His father is a veterinarian." she replied.

...

Another time a young child had a broken hand and I set the bones. The anxious mother asked "Will she be alright?" So trying to be reassuring with a little humor, I said, "Yes, she'll be fine, only thing she won't be able to do is to play the piano." The mother became extremely distraught. "Did I say something that upset you?" I said. "Yes, she is studying to be a concert pianist."

...

Usually after completion of surgery we check the patient's blood count before discharge. One lady's count was low, so I told her I going to give her a unit of blood before she left the hospital. She looked at me and said, "What on earth am I going to do with the blood, make sausage?"

...

An arrogant, pompus GE executive was waiting for his wife to be discharged after a hip replacement and he was sitting on the bedside commode. Well, that sure looked funny to me. So I said to him, "Most people usually drop their pants before they use the commode, Mr Fangboner." Needless to say he wasn't very happy with me, but it leveled the playing field, nicely.

...

Old Uncle Beduch finally gave up drinking and Jack Daniels stock price went down 20%.

...

The old priest at St Anthony's was one of the first patients I had in practice. After his visit, he said, "Where is the bill doctor?" I said, "I never charge members of the clergy." "Why thank you very much. Is there anything I can do to help you get started?" "Yes, send me some pateints." I said The next day there was 6 nuns, 3 priests, 2 rabbis and a minister in the waiting room.

...

Pretty "lame" jokes for an orthopedist.

...

During the 30's, cousin Tony Capobianco was sentenced to die in the electric chair for bootlegging and he asked his lawyer for some advice. The lawyer suggested, "Don't sit down" and charged him $2000. Tony replied, "OK, hold my hand."

...

The man in the office asked me if the fracture clavicle (collar bone) would be OK. So stupid me said, "I never saw one that didn't heal." trying to be reassuring. Well as you might expect, it didn't heal and I told the man he needed an operation. So he said to me, "Doctor you told me you never saw one that didn't heal, so that means you never did the operation before?" Swallowing hard, I said, "Yes, but I will ask my partner to help." So I asked my partner Jack, if he had done one? Jack said, "No, but I saw one once in my residency training." I told the patient what he said, and the man said, "OK go ahead, I trust you guys." We did it and it went well and healed. Whew!

BACK TO ONE LINERS...

⅔ of Americans can't do fractions, the other ½ just don't care.

. . .

Also posted by the Vatican newspaper was an release by the Pope Francis saying: All woman that are lying naked in bed with a man, screaming "Oh my God, Oh my God!" That will NOT be considered a form of prayer.

. . .

One good thing about being a narcissist is you don't talk about anybody.

. . .

Donna and I had a nice vacation in Latin America this winter. But I sure wish I studied Latin a little harder in high school, so I could have conversed with the natives.

. . .

A wise man washes his hands when he pees, an even wiser man doesn't pee on his hands.

. . .

I got rid of my masseur today, I didn't like the way she rubbed me.

. . .

One of the statues surrounding the Vatican Plaza came to life. The newspaper said that it was handing out fish, veal and pasta recipes.

. . .

Moses' 7th commandment is: Thou shalt not admit adultery."

...

Recently I saw a lady with two seeing eye dogs, so I said,"What's up with the 2 dogs?" "Oh, one's for reading" she said.

...

My partner's son was a very famous surgeon and wanted him to do his lung resection. I said, "Suppose something happens?" "It won't. I told him if I die, his mother will have to live with his wife and him for the rest of her life."

...

Did you ever stop at a traffic light and see a gal in the adjacent car, putting on her makeup? I have, and often been tempted to yell, "Lady, it's not going to help!"

...

Beduch's children figure when he's ready for a nursing home, they'll just scrub him up a little and drop him off at a exit 9 rest area on the Thruway. It will be close to New York so they can visit him once in a while and I hear the food is great at the Domino's Pizza there.

...

The other possibility for Beduch, is following his hip and knee replacements, cataracts, and heart surgery, his kids will fix him up a little more and see if they can sell him.

...

My grandkids tell me they don't like taking English in school. I told them, "English is important, but music is more importantner."

...

My surgical colleague told me he keeps his shoes well polished so he can look up the nurses dresses. But the nurses got the best of him, they started wearing slacks.

...

Criminal lawyers is that redundant?

...

Uncle Beduch went to claim his social security benefits, but forgot his ID. So the clerk said, "That's ok old timer, just unbutton your shirt and if you have gray hair you qualify." So he did and qualified. Pleased, Beduch went home and told his wife. "It's too bad she didn't ask you to drop your pants, you would gotten disability benefits too." she said.

...

After exhaustive medical tests, I still didn't have the diagnosis. So exasperated, I said, " I'm stumped Mrs. Haribottom, we'll have to wait for the autopsy!" (Naw, I didn't say that)

Jack, a retired surgeon working on your "Funny Bone" to keep you in stitches.

Mrs Generosa Emasculante

If you have endured this far, we are friends. Let me share this last funny true story with you:

. . .

Emergency room call can be very difficult for a physician. All hours of the day and night, holidays, our children's special events, we are expected to be available. My partner was retiring and it was his very last night of ER call. So..... I thought I would have some fun and had my wife call his house pretending to be the doctor's answering service. Donna said, "Doctor Richards we have a very bad school bus accident, there are many children badly injured and we have several open fractures. Would you like me to alert the operating room?" I wish I had a recording of his response. He went "bonkers." He was so upset about his bad luck on his last night of call. Then Donna and I started laughing hysterically. "You got me," he said, quite relieved. Both of us have had many laughs about that story since. It was a "get even" for a practical joke he played on me many years prior that was also very funny. If you know me, ask me about it and I will tell you the story.

. . .

After that last story, I guess I still can remember more than a one liner. Let's see, where did I put my glasses?

The laughs are out there if you are receptive and have an open mind. It really helps to deal with the frustrations of life. I hope you have enjoyed the book and it brightened your life a little. Remember, if you don't laugh it'll back up as gas.